the

POWER

of

USING PAIN

for

PURPOSE

PALMETTO
P U B L I S H I N G
Charleston, SC
www.PalmettoPublishing.com

Paperback ISBN: 979-8-8229-3155-8

the
POWER
of
USING PAIN
for
PURPOSE

Kristina Davidson

Contents

Dedication

I'd like to dedicate this book to the handful of people who are no longer with me to continue celebrating life together as the journey continues. A very special dedication to the patient who never got the chance to read my story to the very end. Your interaction with me meant more to me than anyone will ever truly know. I know you said that I was inspiring; but you were a great inspiration yourself. Even through tough times as your illness progressed, your smile was captivating until the very end.

And to my son, I sincerely hope you never have to work as hard as I did to get here. But I do hope that through me you'll see the value in hard work. Take every opportunity that life presents you when there is a chance to grow. Do not listen to those who say it can't be done. And always believe in yourself, because the only competition lies within the mirror—not the person beside you. Do not ever be afraid to change your perspective if you don't like the current view. Never take time for granted; and don't be afraid to fall. Falling will remind you that there is always a time to get up and keep going.

Preface
A Miracle Is a Work of Heart

To have a testimony, you must first be put to the test. No one likes taking tests; they bring anxiety, uncertainty, and unwanted feelings. But there is no better feeling than being on the other side of the fence to talk about your personal accomplishments, especially when you have been surrounded by people who doubt you or tell you that you can't do it. And that is exactly what this story is about. My life has been full of a lot pain, but gradually over time it revealed an even greater purpose. Pain can either drive you to make terrible decisions that can haunt you, or it can drive you to do better things. I chose to make the best of my cards I was dealt, but I had no idea the purpose that would come along with it. So here's to the girl who once believed she couldn't do it, who learned to surround herself with genuine people and accept nothing less than to achieve more in life.

I can do all things through Christ who strengthens me.—Philippians 4:13.

It took a lot of sacrifice, grit, hard work, determination, and self-discipline to reach this point. You must believe in yourself against all odds. When you fall—because you'll fall more than once—you *will* need people around you who will help you back up. But not only just that, you must realize that there is a lot to learn from a fall. Realize why you fell, take in the perspective of being on your back when you face what is above you, and acknowledge if you got hurt. You may even have to heal, but remember there will always come a time to get up and keep going.

Chapter 1: Introduction
Where It Started

I grew up in Raytown, Missouri, a relatively older small town at the time. I was adopted by my great-grandparents, whom I came to know as my official mom and dad on November 4, 1996. I still have the picture taken at the courthouse of my mom holding me on her left hip and my dad standing on the other side of the judge with the biggest smile on his face. I was raised by them from birth even though my official adoption was two and half years after I was born. My mom was sixty when she adopted me; my dad was sixty-three. That's *six entirely different decades* between us. That provided a lot of benefits, but later, it brought challenges as well.

My mom taught me how to read and write. I may not have been the smartest kid in the class, but my mom definitely invested a lot of time into my education. Maybe she knew more about my future than I ever did because at one point, I couldn't even see living past eighteen, and that's how real this is about to get. I just want to pause for a second and tell you that things *do* get better. You overcome battles you never thought you could fight. You are not alone;

as a matter of fact, you were never alone. As a firm believer in Christ today, I just want to affirm that you can always count on him. Secondly, it is important to have a community behind you. It can be made up of biological family members, friends that become family, coworkers, counselors, adjunct professors, or even strangers. As I look back, there are so many faces that I will never forget, and those interactions will always live within me. There are so many people that I want to thank for being a part of my community who helped me reach my educational goals. But I'll address that more a little later in my story.

I had a relatively stable childhood, and for that, I couldn't be more thankful. Fast forward to twenty-nine years later. I saw a very traditional Christian marriage growing up. My mom tended to the inside of the house while my dad did the exterior. My mom never drove. My dad grilled, but you wouldn't catch him in the kitchen. They each had their role that they had figured out by then, I guess. I was the last child they raised, so as you can imagine, I was very spoiled. They raised four kids together, all of them in their thirties by the time I was adopted. I technically have three older sisters and one older brother, all of whom are over the age of sixty at this time.

While I grew up in a different decade than the rest of them, we all have a few things in common—one being we all attended church in our childhood. Every Sunday morning and Wednesday night, we attended church like clockwork. I was raised in church; I attended Bible quiz, a national girls ministry program called Missionettes, church choir, and youth camps. My mom was very strict, so if she didn't know the parents and if the parents weren't churchgoers, I wasn't allowed to be there. But the truth is, not all churchgoers are pure themselves. The dad of one of my close childhood church friends was a child molester. He went to jail as he should, but unfortunately, that's a memory in my existence. As a parent myself, I understand the great lengths you will go to protect your child.

However, you can't protect your child from everything. You can only keep them protected in a bubble for so long. So you educate your children the best way you know how in the hope that they use those tools in their toolbox when danger presents itself. I wasn't taught all of those tools in childhood; some of those tools came along in young adulthood. But I can look back and respect most of the decisions my parents made or at least understand their thought process in how they wanted to raise me. They had good intentions, as most parents do. However, as I have grown into my own perspective of life, I have had to do some untangling. And that begins here.

Chapter 2: Trauma
The Never-Ending Traumas

I've been overcoming challenges since I was in the womb. Even as a newborn, this continued when I was diagnosed with bacterial meningitis. So in some ways, I guess you could say I was born to naturally be someone who was never going to give up, and I would overcome the challenges I faced ahead.

My childhood was fun to me, even though others may say it was very basic and boring. I had a very structured routine, set bedtimes, and the same prepared meals on the menu. I am one of the last in this millennial generation who could enjoy being outside until the sun started to go down. I knew then I had to come inside, even when I didn't want to, because that was the rule. I always enjoyed playing with the twin boys next door who were about my age. We would always play hide-and-seek and tag and chase each other on our bikes, going wickedly fast down the hill we lived on. I always tried to be as fast or as strong as them. I remember when they got their training wheels off of their bikes—before I did, of course. I begged my dad to take them off because

I knew I was ready. But my dad was so hesitant because he didn't want me to get hurt. I somehow managed to convince him to do it for me, and that was the greatest feeling of independence. I can still remember riding my bike like I was a pro. One thing about me is I have never been afraid to try, even when someone else questions it. This also means I am not afraid to fall.

I enjoyed being outside in the summer with my dad, catching fireflies in jars. I would collect as many as I could. And when I was done, my dad would poke holes in the jar lid so they could still breathe. That is by far my favorite memory with my dad, something incredibly simple that didn't cost much at all and took up a small amount of time in the evening. Because I was adopted by my great-grandparents, I had the opportunity to spend so much time around them. Some might argue maybe too much, but nonetheless, this was a truly beautiful thing as I look back. I can count on one hand how many times I was babysat so my parents could go do what they needed or wanted to do. My mom had separation anxiety from me when I started elementary school, so much so that she went as far as getting a job in the kitchen just to be able to see me during the day. Back then, I was completely annoyed and found it to be embarrassing. Today, I look back and think how appreciative I am to have that memory. Not everyone is lucky enough to have the mom I had, and truly, I am blessed.

When I was around the age of eleven, I graduated the Missionette program at the church I attended with my parents. My navy-blue sash displayed various badges that were sewn on to show the levels of biblical principles that I learned and practiced in my journey. When I graduated, I became an honor star and received a crown. The honor star program showcased the girls who went above and beyond to earn this ceremony that was celebrated at church with friends and family. I wore an all-white dress, and my dad walked me down the aisle to receive my crown. We walked together to the song "Isn't She Lovely" by Stevie Wonder. I can still remember the feeling of joy my dad radiated while walking me down the aisle, just as strong as the harmonica played in that song. I was crowned by the pastor of the church with my parents standing beside me. I remember playing my violin to showcase one of my talents to the audience. After the official ceremony came the reception, where we celebrated with all of our friends and family. I just remember having cake and looking at my table that my family helped decorate with pictures of me throughout my childhood up until that point. It was a great memory for everyone there; they were all so proud of me and my accomplishments.

My parents were supportive of me, loved me, and always kept me safe. They provided me with structure and discipline, things I am so thankful for to this day. My biological mom being a drug addict gave me the opportunity to be raised in a totally different environment than what she would have given me. The doctors actually told my family I would never be able to walk or talk because of the drugs my biological mom took when she was pregnant with me. I have limited memories with her because of the life she lived. But I do appreciate the things she tried to implement to remain in some sort of contact, even if it was random. One time, she showed up at my parents' house with a chocolate ice cream cup just for me. Before I could even take my first bite, the mom who raised me made me throw it away. She feared it would be laced with drugs. And just like that, my feelings were thrown away with that ice cream cup that day. I didn't understand it all back then, but it unfortunately made me feel unwanted and fearful as a child. Her addiction led to multiple hospital visits, jail time, rehabs, broken hearts, family members raising her four daughters, and, eventually, to her death. I now understand the many traumas I did not have to face because of my adoption, but I still felt the hurt from her addictions.

I can still remember receiving her phone calls late at night from jail and never knowing what to say, so I always would just listen. I would always pray for her after the phone call was over, praying she would get her life in order for us to be a real family one day. My memories with her are very limited, but one of my favorite memories that always makes me laugh was when I was with my little half sister. I was in eighth grade at the time, so she would have been in fifth grade or so. She was holding a hair straightener in a way that looked like she had a boner. And me being me, I said, "It looks like you have a boner." So she naturally asked, "What's that?" I told her to go ask our mom, thinking this would be hilarious. One thing about our mom was that she had a very fun and free spirit. So when she went to ask our mom this lovely question, our mom just bluntly stated, "It's when a guy's penis gets hard." And my innocent little sister just said, "Oh, okay," and kept moving.

Eighth grade was a fun year for me. I loved going to school on Fridays because they always had donuts. Middle school academics were challenging, but I loved learning and trying new things. I had really great friends in middle school who are still a part of my life to this day. My best friend and I met in sixth grade, and by the time eighth grade came around, we were always talking about what our future would look like. We shared a lot of the same interests at the time, including orchestra, but she was so much more outgoing than I was. She brought me out from under the rock I seemed to live under my whole life. She changed my music interests from the Jump 5 group to Ciara—what a necessary change.

I had everything that an average thirteen-year-old girl could truly hope for. A happy, healthy home environment, shopping sprees with friends, volleyball, school events, and thinking about what the future would hold. I was a very joyful kid, always was. But on March 27, 2008, my whole life changed and flipped upside down. The previous night, we had attended church just like normal.

My youth group happened to get out earlier than the adult church, so I had gone into the gymnasium to play with my friends. On this particular night, I had invited a friend with me to church. If you really know me, you know I was always inviting friends to church. When the adult church was over, my parents entered the gymnasium to let us know they were ready to leave. I wanted to stay with my friends for as long as possible, so I had asked for more time. My parents agreed and left to go pull up the car to wait. Some time went by, and my dad came up to the exterior doors of the gymnasium to knock on the door.

On this particular night, some boys who were about my age had been seen forcefully kicking those doors open. When my dad knocked, one of those teenage boys decided to kick open that heavy metal door. My dad fell back and hit his head on the concrete as a result. There weren't a lot of witnesses to this incident, and let me be clear here. This was not a complete accident. It was an extremely poor choice made by a young teenage boy that cost someone else their life—an extremely catastrophic, devastating, and life-changing event for everyone involved.

When my dad fell, there was no blood at the scene. He was able to get up with some help. I was notified of the event and immediately went outside to check on him. All I knew was that my dad was hit by the door, which caused him to fall and hit his head. I watched my dad stumble around the car with a hand on his head while he kept saying "Jesus, help me" on the way to the driver's seat. Remember, my mom never drove.

I had taken some science courses by this time and knew to ask some cognitive questions to see if he could still understand what I was saying. On the drive home, I asked my dad questions like, "What sound does a cow make? What sound does a pig make?" Apparently these were my alert and oriented questions at the time. And as he would make the correct corresponding sound, we were all able to laugh in this moment. But this would be the last time we would all laugh together.

My gut knew something was not right, just from the way I observed my dad walking and watching him hold his head, clearly in pain. I begged my mom to take him to the ER that night. I even went as far as calling my older siblings to tell them what happened to try to help convince our mom to take him to the ER. My mom never drove; she wasn't getting out for this. She didn't think anything of it. She honestly thought he would be okay and we should just pray about it. And for that reason, she didn't call for an ambulance when we got home that night. About 4:30 the next morning, I woke up to ambulance lights and paramedics in my parents' room. My dad was face down on the floor, completely unconscious. This was the most gut-wrenching day of my entire life to this day. I didn't eat that day, and so many tears were shed.

The doctors told us that he had suffered a subdural hematoma and that the blood pooled down to his brain stem. My dad died later that night on March 27, 2008. I was only thirteen years old. Everything went downhill from there. I did not return to school for nearly a week. This happened to be around the time of state MAP testing, so I knew I eventually had to go back. And coming back to school was not easy. Everyone wanted to ask me how he died. I was given a giant card signed by all of these same kids, asking me for details I could barely share without shedding tears while my voice cracked. I went from being a straight-A student (for the most part) on the honor roll every semester for perfect attendance to someone who no longer cared to prioritize school.

Four days later was the funeral. The very next day was the burial. His funeral was the largest funeral I have ever attended. And maybe I felt that way because I was now suddenly someone who was sitting in the front row instead of somewhere in the back. Maybe that was because I had to stand in line to greet everyone who came down to give my family their condolences, even when I had a puffy and red face, even when I couldn't breathe because my chest was so tight. My head hurt from all of the crying, but yet here I was.

One of those individuals in the line was the boy who caused this funeral in the first place. My dad had forgiven him. My mom had forgiven him. I had said I had forgiven him too. But was I still angry? Absolutely, and that emotion stayed with me for years to come. And it came in a lot of behaviors that some saw firsthand. But regardless, my dad's funeral was filled with so many people who loved him, who loved me. He used to keep a few wallet-sized pictures of me in his wallet. Every time he would go to open that soft, worn-down leather wallet, I would find myself always with him. Everywhere he went, I was right there with him. Every night before he used to go to bed, I would make sure to give him a hug, even if he forgot. I would go into his room and give him a hug and tell him, "Good night, Dad. I love you." So when my son always comes into my room with a hug because I forgot, it always takes me back to that one familiar soft place in my heart where I shared this exact same love for my dad.

The one word that really stood out to me at his funeral was the word "legacy." One thing about my dad is he *never* knew a stranger. I can remember him sitting on a random bench while he would wait for my mom to be done shopping at the Bannister Mall before it was torn down a few years later. He would strike up a conversation with anybody who sat down next to him. I truly do believe he touched so many souls throughout his lifetime, and that was reflected in the amount of seats that were taken at his funeral. He left a legacy for so many people to carry on with them in their hearts wherever life would take them next.

The burial was a super cold day on the last day of March. I remember we all went to First Watch to have breakfast after. I don't know why it's a tradition to eat when someone is mourning. I am not one of those people who eat more when they are emotional; I am the exact opposite. I didn't know that then; I was just hurting. But I was extremely lucky enough to have some of the best friends in middle school who were by my side through it all with me. I would not be here today without them. My dad was like a dad to my friends; his love always extended to them. He enjoyed taking them to lunch with us after church on Sundays. Life took us all different places, but I have not forgotten who each one of you was to me in that moment. Some of those same individuals who went to breakfast that day with my family stayed on that bumpy rollercoaster ride with me, a ride that I did not ask to be on.

I often wonder how that boy's life played out, and I mean from the *bottom of my heart, I do not wish any harm to him or his parents*. I just experienced *so much pain while being so young* in such a traumatic way that is deeply rooted inside of me, like an internal tattoo that can never be removed. I've just had to learn how to keep going despite any emotion that came along my journey. But life doesn't stop going, even when your world seems to have come to a complete stop. Even though summer is known for sunshine, the one in 2008 was particularly gray for me.

That summer was extremely hard for me. I spent a lot of it indoors, and I know now that is a huge indicator for me that my mental health is not up to par. I love being outside in the summer. I love the sun hitting my skin, being near a pool, and just living in the moment. I had spent every summer up until 2008 outside soaking up the sun, enjoying every single minute of it. I have so many memories at the local water park in Raytown with my best friend and her cousin. No wonder that is where I ended up working as a lifeguard for my first job years later.

While I was dealing with the loss of my father, my biological mother somehow managed to get in touch with my biological father. He was living in Kansas City and wanted to see me. At this time and to my knowledge, I had never met him before. It was such an awkward time for me, as I had just lost the dad who raised me; I had conflicting feelings as it was. She and my grandma made this arrangement for me to meet him. I met him at Chili's, and I don't remember much from that experience, but I do remember he showed me a picture of his other two kids. They looked to be about my age, a brother and a sister. My biological dad is Cuban and has a very thick accent, which makes it extremely hard to hold conversations with him. After we had lunch, we took a picture together, and he handed me $100. Social media was not as big as it is today, but he did give me his phone number. We had a few phone calls after that meetup; however, the phone calls stopped shortly after. I never knew why or what happened. It was like I was just ghosted. At the time, I never really knew why he wasn't a part of my life to begin with or even if he wanted to be. I had always assumed he didn't want me. I felt angry for a long time after, and just like that, the picture we took disappeared.

The mother who raised me was extremely upset that I had gone to see my biological father, because this meeting was completely set up behind her back. At the time, coming from a child's perspective, I couldn't understand why this would make her so upset. So back then, it caused a lot of turmoil in our relationship. It caused a lot of family drama between the three generations of women as well, and as a result, I felt the heat from that drama. It only internalized more feelings of anger for me that summer.

My freshman year, I decided to continue orchestra and volleyball. Volleyball was a great outlet for me to let out my anger when spiking a ball or challenging myself to get better at something. I enjoyed spending time with new friend groups that year and exploring high school courses. Looking back, freshman year was probably the most fun for me because of how new everything was. Sophomore year, I started to struggle. I decided to not continue orchestra at this time, and I did not make the volleyball team. However, it made me want to get better for the tryouts next year. So I convinced my mom to let me play off-season volleyball, and I got straight to work. I wasn't going to waste her money on this expensive off-season.

By the time junior year rolled around, I was really struggling in academics and attendance. But I did make the JV volleyball team and always looked forward to that aspect of my life. I was struggling so much that one of my teachers noticed a change and attempted to talk to me about my failing grade in that particular class. This was just the beginning of that year.

My best friend had me move in with her with the hopes of keeping me on the straight and narrow to stay in school. It helped a lot, but I eventually decided to go back to my mom's house and went downhill again. I missed almost an entire week of school but decided to go back on Friday that week. I got suspended that same Friday, which led to me having entirely too much time on my hands. I decided to spend that newfound quality time with my boyfriend at the time. Fast forward eight weeks or so later when I found out we were pregnant at the beginning of the last month of my junior year. My lack of attendance plus the five-day suspension did not meet the newly enforced attendance policy. This was crazy, because, when I look back, my school did not have an attendance policy prior to my junior year, so all of my other credits were at least valid if I passed the course up until that point. My junior year did not look great on paper at all, but lucky for me, I attended summer school almost every summer, so I was ahead of the game in terms of credits.

That summer of 2011 was not an easy one. My biological mom was the only family member who was completely ecstatic about my pregnancy and didn't hold any judgment. What I needed in that moment was all the support I could get. I luckily had my best friend and her mom, who showed the most loving and graceful support I have ever experienced even to this day. I can still remember sitting on the porch and my best friend's mom asking me, "What is it that *you* want to do? Not your family. But you?" And those were the words I needed to hear to help support my decision. I had my first doctor's appointment at eleven weeks. While there were so many emotions up in the air, my one hope was that this first grandchild of hers would finally make her turn her drug addict life around. I was so excited for her to find out the sex of the baby; she was hoping for a healthy baby boy. However, on July 14, 2011, I was at my best friend's house when I received the phone call that my biological mom had been murdered. She was unfortunately stabbed to death in a Kansas City motel. I was only seventeen years old at the time. I was crying so hysterically, my best friend drove me across the state line to be with my devastated family members in Kansas. My pregnancy was an emotionally challenging one as I was dealing with the unknown future, losing my biological mom, and knowing I had my senior year starting up in just a few short weeks.

Like most teenagers, I did not want to miss out on my senior year despite being pregnant. I showed up to my classes as much as I could because I was determined to finish so I could walk with my graduating class and get my diploma. I was already in the dead parent club for losing my dad, and now I found myself enrolled in the teen mom club as well. With both clubs, I was forced to attend meetings at school, which included talking about our feelings; this became even more traumatizing for me. I absolutely hated being in both clubs. But just like attending those clubs, I attended my classes that fall. Luckily, my due date was during Christmas break, so I was able to finish that semester with no problems. My OBGYN talked me into a scheduled induction so that we could avoid giving birth during the holidays. My mom wasn't even planning on coming to the hospital for my delivery, but my best friend's mom made sure she didn't miss this moment. I am not sure if it was because of how my mom felt about my pregnancy or if she was just afraid to drive across the state line. But regardless, that hurt my feelings. Thank you to my best friend's mom, who made sure she was there on a day I needed her.

So on December 20, 2011, I was induced, which also turned out to be my last day of finals. My best friend showed up immediately after she finished taking her tests. I was pretty much just hanging out with everyone up until it was time to give birth. Everyone joked with me that I was going to have a baby that looked Asian, and they weren't wrong! I am very thankful that this was a healthy pregnancy and no complications occurred during delivery. I now know how dangerous it can be to be induced when you actually don't need to be. I remember not knowing if I wanted to have an epidural and the nurses convincing me that time was running out to make that decision and that I should go ahead with it. I wasn't able to move my legs for several hours after the epidural, and that was so traumatic for me as I was so young and had no idea what was really going on. But as time went on, I regained feeling in my legs and got the strength to get up out of bed.

The next few months were tough, but so many beautiful memories were created during this time. My boyfriend at the time and I moved into our apartment just days before I was induced. We had a lot of unpacking and settling down to do as the next few weeks went on. I remember going over to my mom's house with my newborn son. This was where I saw a miracle come around when I needed her support. She fell in love with her first great-great-grandchild. She loved rocking him and holding him. I am so grateful to have those memories of them. My mom helped watch my son while I finished taking a few courses my last semester. She also watched him while I worked a few jobs as time went on. As he grew, so did her love for him. I made sure I captured as many pictures and videos as I could because I knew she wouldn't be around forever. That day came so much sooner than I realized it would. During the late spring of 2014, my mom was diagnosed with abdominal cancer. This was so devastating as she was my last lifeline of support as a parent. She tried to fight it with chemo, and just a few short months later, she passed away on July 14, 2014, when I was only twenty years old. However, my story didn't just end here. It kept going, and I am going to tell you how it got better, even when numerous challenges presented themselves.

It is a complete miracle to even be here to tell my testimony, as it is filled with multiple devastating traumas. Pain can take you so many different places over time. There's not one emotion I haven't felt. But by the grace of God, I am strong enough to still be standing, and I am here to tell you that if I can do it, so can you.

Chapter 3: The Journey
Dating Before You Know Yourself

My first serious relationship was my high school boyfriend, the one I had a baby with at seventeen years old. As you can imagine, we struggled tremendously in so many ways. We both made a ton of mistakes that led to resentment, unhealed wounds, and guilt. He was nineteen and had just barely graduated high school at the time. I was a senior finishing out my last year while raising our newborn. I thought the biggest challenges I would face ahead would be waking up in the middle of the night to change diapers and feed the baby, but that was nothing compared to what else I was going through. Nobody really prepared me for the postpartum depression that came. I was in a very dark space for months. I would call my best friend crying, not even really fully understanding what I was going through. I had heard about it before, of course. But somehow I thought I wouldn't be affected by it because it couldn't be worse than the depression I was already in, right? Wrong! I give myself a lot of grace now as I look back at how I treated myself and others while I simply attempted to survive.

My boyfriend had cars on and off just as much as our relationship was up and down. One day we were together, the next we weren't. We were constantly fighting, and the fact that I was the only one who consistently had a car only added to the stress. Now this chapter is not about blame or shame; it's about fundamentally laying a foundation for how I was able to overcome those challenges to be where I am now. He wasn't the most reliable father at this time; he wasn't the one that I *needed* him to be. Considering I had such a stable upbringing and exceptional father when it came to safety and security, I needed that back then. I didn't know it as much as I do now, but my boyfriend at the time wasn't able to give me that. And that is his own story to tell. I just want to share how this affected me.

Our lows were low. We didn't know how to love each other, even if we said those three words to one another. With our first apartment together, he was the one who signed the lease because he was over the age of eighteen. I just happened to legally be an occupant because of that. This was my only saving grace in this moment, because over time, he stopped paying for that apartment, which then ended up in an eviction. Evictions stay on your record for seven years, making it extremely hard to rent during those next chapters of your life. He already relied heavily on me for my car, so it then became harder on us that I had to carry the weight for any future rental properties. At the time, my credit was not the greatest, and we did not have a ton of money. Neither one of us was in our careers; we simply had disposable jobs. I luckily had WIC services when my son was young. I didn't know what that service was until I needed it. Someone had told me I would qualify and benefit, and just like that, I applied for it. I remember they supplied me with so many gallons of milk every month that I would end up giving milk away to someone else who needed it. We paid out of pocket for daycare, which seemed expensive back then. However, compared to daycare prices today, that's a joke. Prior to being evicted from our first apartment, we, of course, got into a fight. He kicked me out of the apartment, and I subsequently found myself back at my mom's for the time being. At one point, I moved out again and got another apartment. It became too expensive, and I ended up back at home yet again. This was a routine pattern, something that I later found to be a generational curse in my family, but I'll address that later.

At the beginning of summer 2014, I signed a lease on a sketchy apartment in south Kansas City. This was the last apartment that my boyfriend and I shared together. Just a few short weeks after we moved in, my mom passed away. Every once in a while, I would go back to the only house I grew up in for seventeen years of my life, but it was now completely empty. Silence can be peaceful, but it can also be excruciatingly painful when you are hurting. All of the memories flooded back to me. Hearing my dad mow the lawn in the summertime, smelling the lilacs my mom would plant in the spring. Hearing my dad walk up and down the halls with the change in his pockets that would move around with every step he took. Smelling the nasty odor of vinegar when it came time for my mom to do her annual spring cleaning. Smelling the baby's breath tree in the backyard and immediately feeling allergy season upon us. Or even just hearing the kitchen clock tick in silence in the evenings when it was time to turn the TV off before bed. I realized I would never watch my mom wake up again to religiously watch the 6:00 a.m. Fox 4 news daily. When my dad died, my mom quickly got rid of all of his belongings. And that was triggering for me. I couldn't understand why anyone would do that. The walls were not the same when they no longer carried the sound. The once messy closets had become empty. And the space that was no longer filled now felt lonely.

One of the things I did inherit from my dad was his wedding band, which I still wear faithfully to this day. I have a few other things, but that is the most important one to me. I was a daddy's girl without a shadow of a doubt, so my family knew it would mean so much to give me that. When family members die, it's very easy for everyone to get greedy quickly. Everyone wants to fight over who should get what and when to sell the house. My family was no different.

Fast forward a few months after settling into that sketchy apartment. A shooting literally occurred in my back-yard. My boyfriend, our son, and I were hanging out upstairs in bed, watching TV together. All of a sudden we hear *pop pop pop pop pop*, and our apartment lit up so bright, like lightning had just struck our windows! My boyfriend imme-diately yelled to get down on the ground, quickly turned off all of the lights and TV, and told me to stay quiet. All I can remember were tears streaming down my face, completely afraid that this was the last time we would all be together.

Growing up in Raytown, I was accustomed to hearing gunshots go off, but they were probably miles away. The sound was always loud enough to know a gunshot had gone off, but it wasn't close enough for me to really live in fear. This was the first time I had ever been so close to multiple bullets being fired. I knew in that moment if I survived that night, I was not finishing out this lease. I did not care where I went, but I knew safety was an absolute priority. The next morning, I told my leasing office I was moving out. They tried to argue with me that I couldn't leave the premises. Me being me, I said, "Oh yeah? Watch me."

A few weeks went by, and to no one's surprise, my boyfriend and I were once again arguing and breaking up for the 103,943,752nd time. But this time, I felt it in my soul that if we were going to break up *again*, I was officially going to stay gone. And that is exactly what happened. This didn't make it in any easier on me; I knew I had to still get out of this sketchy apartment situation alone. At the time, I was lucky enough to work with some men who helped me move my belongings from that sketchy apartment back into the house I grew up in—this would be the last time I would ever live there.

That leasing office was *not* happy with me, but guess what? I was off the premises just like I said I would be! I ended up being able to break my lease, but I had to work extra hours to be able to do that because that was not a part of my monthly bills. This was just the beginning of where I needed so much more help than I could really ask for, understand, process, and even be grateful for at the time.

Now I was really single and really feeling all of the overwhelming emotions along with it. I was twenty years old at this point, my son was three years old, and I knew nothing about being a single mom. My parents who raised me had a solid marriage, and all I knew was to eventually get married. I watched all of my older sisters by adoption get married, even get divorced, and then get married again. My thought process at this time was I needed a man. And boy, did that turn out to be wrong—but just wait for the next season of my life to unravel.

One of the men who helped me move from that sketchy apartment back into the house I initially grew up in became my boyfriend just a few months later. He had a job and a car, and I thought that would provide the stability I absolutely needed in a relationship. I thought that's what made a man a *man*, just simply having a sense of responsibility. By then, I was accustomed to working two different jobs. I usually had a serving job for quick cash. I absolutely loved the time I spent serving tables. Even when people got hangry and gave you attitudes and tipped based off that, I still loved being a server. Some of the most down-to-earth people work in the front and back of the house of a restaurant. This made for great friendships, even years later for me. At that time, I also had a full-time job where I worked with my new boyfriend. Both of us knew we wouldn't make this job a career for either one of us, but it served its purpose at that time. So I worked my typical nine-to-five job and served some weeknights and a lot of weekends. Why? Because I needed money to survive. I didn't have any parents anymore, and my baby daddy was not making sure we were always going to be taken care of. That was solely on me, even in this new relationship. I still had to pull my own weight, which included paying my half of bills, and so I began to work toward bettering my situation for my son.

In the midst of this new relationship, my family began to talk about the need to sell the house I was now living in. But I also wasn't the only one living there; my older brother by adoption lived in the basement. He had been residing there for over a decade at this point. Due to his own life choices, he consequently ended up back at the parents' house as a middle-aged adult. See a pattern here yet? That made two out of the five kids my parents raised living in the house and wanting to keep it. The other two adult children wanted to sell it. Well, what about the fifth adult child? She was removed from my parents' will, so she had zero say in whether the property remained in the family or if it hit the market. Sounds pretty harsh, huh? This wasn't even the ugliest part yet. (Kids, be nice to your parents as you get older because that can be a harsh reality). We sold this house in 2015 for a ballpark price of $105,000.

Today in the year 2024, this house is worth over $100,000 more than the price we sold it for. Knowing what I know now, it was a huge mistake to sell our piece of pie in the real estate game. But because of my older adult siblings with their perspective and their own current realities, they sold it. My parents had owned this house for decades; it was paid off before we all even inherited it. So even if it did need a new roof or a new HVAC system or it had issues with plumbing, we could have collectively worked as a team to figure it out. God did not put us on this earth to pit us against one another to end up only working against ourselves. Let that sit for a minute and simmer in your mind. They let their fear of the unknown along with their personal opinions outweigh their faith in God.

While we were getting this house on the market ready to sell, I now had to move yet again. At the time, my new boyfriend and I decided to get a place together. He was tired of renting with friends, and I now needed a roof over my head. This seemed to be the right direction. So I moved across the state line from Missouri to Kansas, which was where I desired to live if I was staying in the Midwest. It was a big mistake for me to move in with another man, but a great lesson was learned. His lease was not quite up yet, so I stayed in the rental with him and his friend for several weeks. I think this was quite the adjustment for everyone, including my three-year-old son. We ended up renting an apartment that was near our job, which made things convenient for me. I learned that I enjoyed being close to work; I did not like driving long distances every single day. And lucky for me because this all came into play when I got into a car accident that ended up totaling my car.

I've always had a car, even before I technically received my license on my sixteenth birthday. I still remember this like yesterday. I was at school when my mom called me.

She asked, "Kristina, what color did you say that you wanted your car to be again?"

And I replied, "Silver, I want a silver car."

She said, "Well, that's too bad. It's blue!" She was giggling with pure giddiness. That's the day I was a new proud owner of a 2008 blue Ford Focus. This was a very nice car for a first car, and it subtly showed in the parking lot of the school I attended. I drove all through the streets of Raytown at ungodly hours in this thing. We had a lot of first memories. I actually drove it once before I got my license. I remember my mom was gone for the day, and I wanted to go to Chipotle with my friend after school—and so we did. I don't know if she ever knew I did that or if she even noticed. But I can't tell her, and I can't ask her since she's no longer with me. But that's just one of the many memories I have in that car. My friends have even more memories with me, because I was always pulling up somewhere with my music turned all the way up. A friend's dad once joked with me that my baby was going to born deaf because of how loud my music always was. And while he was not born deaf, he sure does have selective hearing!

When I was nineteen years old, I decided I wanted a new car. I knew nothing about cars. That is still true to this day, but I have gotten a lot better. All I had was memories of the different cars my parents had. I can remember being a small child sitting in between my parents while my dad drove our little red family truck that was a stick shift. This truck was so small that every time he switched gears, I remember the feeling of the stick hitting my knee. Meanwhile, they also had the two older, ugly boat-looking Buicks. I just knew I didn't want any of those vehicles that I saw in my parents' driveway growing up. Instead, I decided I wanted a brand-new 2014 black Hyundai Elantra. Looking back, I know how dumb a decision this was, but back then, I wanted it, and I was not stopping until I got it. The car I traded in was paid off, meaning I paid *zero* car payments on this vehicle. I traded that unknown freedom in for a brand-new car that came with payments I had to make for the first time. I didn't have good credit, and so I needed my mom to cosign on it. I had messed up my credit before I actually even knew what it was. Oh, but just wait, there is a whole chapter coming on that. I don't even know why my mom agreed to do that because love doesn't justify a dumb decision like that as I look back on that day. But nonetheless, this taught me how a monthly obligation worked, late payments and all.

Now let's get caught back up to the totaling of my brand-new car. For over three years, I had always had a vehicle, so on the day that my world came to an abrupt halt, I was just in shock. It was raining on that day. I was on my lunch break, going to get food. Basically what happened was a car was turning left, and they couldn't see me coming because of the backed up lane across from them. Even though it wasn't my fault, I hit this car at almost forty miles per hour. I am a religious seatbelt wearer for the most part, and luckily, I was wearing it that day. The cops who showed up told me that they saw a similar accident where the driver went through the windshield. They were not wearing their seatbelt but were driving at the same speed I was in my car accident. I was scared to drive for months after this took place. It was traumatizing to me, especially when it rained. But I couldn't just not drive anymore; that wasn't an option. I had to learn to overcome that new fear.

The car that I hit went flying into someone's front yard. My car T-boned the passenger side where a husband was sitting. He ended up with fractured ribs; his wife, who was the driver, was okay. Someone who witnessed the accident immediately came over to me to ask if I was okay. My airbags had deployed—my very first serious car wreck. I just remember shaking in absolute shock. I didn't know who to call first. Obviously 911, but that was the first time I realized in real time that I couldn't just call my mom and tell her I needed help. Even if it was just emotional support, I needed her.

I didn't know it then, but as I look back, it all makes a lot more sense. Everyone says it's either fight-or-flight mode, but for me, it has always been *freeze*. And I hate that is my response to trauma. But nine out of ten times, that's always my freaking response. I'll circle back to trauma responses later, I promise. But as time went on, I had more problems arising. I had only had this new vehicle for a little over one year. At the time of the car accident, I was still on my mom's car insurance policy. Another beautiful thing my mom did for me was always pay my car insurance. After she passed away, I now had that baton, but I remained on the same policy. Well, when I called to let my car insurance know about the accident, they also let me know I was getting dropped from their policy because I was under the age of twenty-one and could not be on my own policy until I reached that age. I was literally less than two months from turning twenty-one years old, and they dropped me like I was hot.

I naturally called around, checking other policies to compare prices. I was looking at $300 a month on the cheap end to have car insurance. Keep in mind I still had my half of bills to pay, my three-year-old who had daycare fees, and any monthly or past obligations to still pay for as well. My boyfriend at the time offered to put me on his car insurance because it was significantly cheaper for me. And I was thankful for that; I truly was—until he weaponized that against me as the years went by. Let me be extremely clear here, though. It started off as helping until it became controlling. When you help someone, you do it with good intentions. You don't help someone and then throw it in their face constantly and tell them, "You can't afford your own car insurance without me." At that point, it is no longer helping; it is indeed controlling, and this was just one of many things that he dangled in my face all of the time, even after we had officially broken up and gone our separate ways.

In the meantime, I needed a car. So I went to a rental car company and was told I needed a credit card. Well, I didn't have one. I somehow managed to bypass that and get the rental. But that same week, I also applied for my first credit card because I didn't want to be in a situation where I couldn't help myself. I knew nothing about credit cards. I didn't even know the differences between the different types of cards or the annual fees that some came with. By the grace of God, my best friend's mom cosigned on another car for me once I found one. At this point, I knew a few things about how cars depreciate quickly. So I chose a smarter option, and I ended up with a newer but used Honda Civic. I did make every single car payment on time; having a cosigner who was practically family to me really helped me learn responsibility. The day that I paid that off (and I did so six months early—yay me!), I can't tell you how proud of myself I was. The weight had finally been lifted off of my shoulders. I never wanted to mess up her future endeavors that she needed to use her credit for. At the time that she signed for me, my best friend was in her third year of college at University of South Florida. We toured that college our junior year together; we had plans of potentially going off to the beach and living our best lives. Even though I knew I did not have a high enough ACT score to get in, nor did I want to study for that exam to aim higher, I also knew I didn't want to leave my mom yet because I knew my time with her would be limited. And I was right; she passed away just two summers after we graduated high school. Nonetheless, my best friend knew a part of my heart was always in Florida.

Two weeks after I bought this car, I ended up road-tripping down to New Orleans to meet up with my best friend to celebrate our twenty-first birthdays together.

We spent a weekend there and then drove down to Tampa, Florida, for a few more days, and my heart felt like it was back home. Later that same year, the house we put on the market finally sold. That feeling that I no longer had a home to go back to if a relationship got rocky solidified. And that really sank in for me. During this time, I was a server on the side, and I remember one of the dishwashers had kept approaching me, asking me the same damn question: "When are you going to go back to school?" He had a sixteen-year-old daughter that I reminded him of. And I just wish today I could give that man a hug, because he was unknowingly prophesying to me. My education ended up saving my life. But it was not an easy route getting there.

I used some of the money from my portion of the house sale to get back into school. I had attempted some courses right out of high school at a local community college. However, the timing just was not right for me, and I did not have the necessary self-discipline to keep going. So while I did initially have some financial aid, I somehow managed to end two or three semesters with failing grades on my transcript. And I also left a remaining balance for books that I had to pay off before I could go back to school again. This time around, I wanted to take things seriously and finish with a degree. I knew I wanted to start at a totally different community college, so I applied to the one in Johnson County. I had to pay for my first semester out of pocket; there were some issues from my prior academics that required me to appeal if I wanted to get financial aid again. This time, I knew I was not playing any games; no one was going to keep me from graduating. I bought my MacBook Air laptop that I still have and am using to write this book. This laptop traveled with me to a few on-site classes, but mainly it was with me at home doing online courses. I tried to take as many courses as I could handle while working two jobs the entire time I was in school.

By the time I was starting the prerequisites, I enrolled in a six-week CNA program with a server friend. We had no idea what we were getting ourselves into, and I still appreciate him so much to this day. He really made that experience fun for me and something to look forward to. I ended up quitting my nine-to-five job, as I figured out this schedule was not designed for me. I applied to some local hospitals and attended a few interviews. I ended up getting the position as a CNA at my number one pick for employment, and that really changed everything for me. I am so incredibly thankful for that door being opened for me. I had no idea how much perspective, incredibly great friendships, and mentorship that would come along with working there.

I was hired on nights on a step-down critical care floor. I eventually enrolled my son in their daycare when he was four years old. I would work 7:00 p.m. to 7:00 a.m., drive home to pick up my son, and then take him to daycare at the same site that I just left so I could sleep for four hours. I couldn't afford more than that, as his daycare was literally nearly half of my hourly rate as a CNA. I would then get back up and go pick him up to then either go back to sleep, study, or attend a class. And odds were I had to go back to work again that night. I did all of this for three years while trying to get into nursing school. I worked as a CNA, and I served a few nights a week while trying to maintain mainly As and a few Bs because getting into nursing school is competitive.

The first year I applied, I was twenty spots away from getting in on the wait list. That disappointment only made me work harder. I applied the following year but still was on the wait list. It was hard watching all of these nursing students come in their JCCC scrubs at the hospital where I worked, all the while hoping I would be next. The issue with applying to nursing schools is that each program has its own set of requirements. One school may require A&P, one math course, two English, and so on, while the next may have all that and then some. On top of that, science courses expire five years after taking them; then you have to retake them. Plus, they each had their own entry exam that you had to get a certain score on or above to even be considered, and those entry exams cost money to take. So this meant I was not only on a pressed timeline, but I also was on a budget. I was trying to be extremely cost-effective at this point. I had benefited from financial aid and scholarships, but I didn't have extra funds to take multiple exams to just *attempt* to get into a nursing program.

After the second year of not getting into the nursing associates program, I decided the following: *You are going to apply to be a LPN as well as a RN, and let's just see if you get into either program.* I had no desire to work as a LPN, because I didn't want to be limited to working in nursing homes and clinics. I knew I wanted to be a RN as the final goal. But I really admired a friend I worked with because she was so transparent about going from LPN and bridging to RN. I quickly realized this just was another way to do it. Now there were a few hoops to get into that program, including an interview process that affected your chances of being accepted. And I thank God every day I shifted to that mindset, because on that third year of applying to nursing programs, I finally received the letter that said, *Congratulations, you've been accepted!* If you have ever been a single mom or hustled hard to get where you wanted to go, you know all of the feels that come with this territory.

By the time I was starting the full-time LPN program, my son was in first grade. Luckily, my school schedule was pretty aligned with his school schedule. I didn't need to rely so much on friends and family to help during this time in terms of school. This program was only a fall and spring semester. For some reason, I thought it would be a great idea to take college algebra while I was in the LPN program; however, it had to be completed prior to starting the bridge program. I took a self-paced college algebra course that was intended to be only nine months long. Self-paced does include a stop date, believe it or not. I took pharmacology during the first semester, and I was able to challenge the medication test at the end to receive my CMA. I passed that and took on third job as a Certified Medication Aide while I was in the spring semester. I did not work full-time hours in any clinical setting while I was in nursing school; I only worked as needed. That was the one benefit that I loved while working in the medical field. It makes it easy if you need flexible schedules. I didn't plan on working much over Christmas break, because I planned to go see my best friend and her new baby girl who had been born in October. That is the one downside to nursing school; a lot of major events get missed because you can't just take off. There are no Paid Time Off requests. If I remember right, I think you could miss one clinical in the entire program. While attending lectures was somewhat optional, it didn't benefit you as a student to not show up.

Somewhere in the middle of spring, applications began for the LPN-to-RN bridge program. This was again a highly selective program, and they only took twelve students. We had approximately twenty-four students in the LPN program, and not everyone applied to go on. However, I was still competing against other LPN graduates from other schools. A few weeks went by, and I found out I was wait-listed. However, I was so stressed out with school at the time that this didn't faze me. While I was disappointed to some degree, I was perfectly fine with working as a LPN that summer and taking some more prerequisites. I was still taking college algebra at this point; it had been seventeen months. Now you are probably asking how and why.

Shortly after my first semester of nursing school, my best friend's baby died of SIDS after only being here sixty-eight days. This was incredibly devastating in so many ways, and it marked a pivotal moment in time for everyone who felt that loss. My plane ticket was already booked for my son, my boyfriend, and me to go down for vacation, which included Disney World and meeting the baby girl I considered my niece. Our trip now included attending her funeral. That was the first baby's funeral I have ever attended. And if you are someone who can relate, you understand that this loss hits differently than losing an older adult. This was a really dark time and yet, I still had to show up for my kid to take him to Disney for his first time. I cannot tell you how hard an internal struggle it was to be in the "happiest place on earth" for kids while only thinking about my best friend's and her husband's aching hearts.

This loss was significant for everyone. It was my best friend's first baby. Her pregnancy included me in a few different moments in time even though we lived in different states. She had flown down to KC to celebrate Easter and her newly announced pregnancy with her family earlier that year. I had the opportunity to watch my best friend and her husband enjoy some of the most unique and intimate moments of pregnancy. This continued even after she was born thanks to FaceTime technology. She was such a happy baby who loved skin-to-skin contact with her mom and dad. I only had the opportunity to feel a few kicks while she was still in the womb, but I'll never forget the absolute joy she brought everyone; even if it was just through a camera. She will always be loved, remembered, and honored as she left a lasting imprint on my heart along with those of many others as well. The community that swarmed in to support this devastated couple extended far beyond anything I have ever seen in my life. They became an entire family to me as well as time went on. I can't thank these individuals enough who were able to support my best friend at a time when I could no longer physically be there. Reality sank in when I had to fly back to KC to resume where my life had left off.

When I came back from Christmas break, I knew I owed many explanations to my college algebra teacher. I had already pushed out my self-paced course prior to all of that tragedy because I knew the weeks leading up to finals were going to be stressful enough. I had hit pause on that course. By the time January came around, it had been several months since I really touched that class. This course was online, so I had never really met the teacher. We only touched base via emails, so I knew this exchange was going to suck.

I had to explain my whole situation, and I did not want to talk about it. This particular teacher looked like she would have never given me the time of day, but she was retiring that semester, and all of her cares were depleted. She graciously extended my course, which is how this became a seventeen-month self-paced class. And just to sum up how this class ended up going, I maintained a grade just high enough on all of the exams and homework collectively that I knew I could go into that final and bomb it. I signed my name and attempted the first problem. Then I picked up the packet and flipped through the numerous pages and said, "Absolutely not." I turned it in with one problem being complete—yes, that is how drained nursing school had me feeling.

I passed college algebra with a C, and *I am telling you, I never* wanted to take another math class again. This was funny, because I still had statistics, but luckily, that class was much easier. But that college algebra prerequisite came in very handy, as time would tell. I was wait-listed for the bridge program, but just a few short days after that wait-list was published, a spot opened up for me! I was bridging that summer immediately after I finished my LPN, which meant in exactly one more year, I would be a RN—finally.

A spot opened up for one of my really good friends in the LPN program who had also been wait-listed! We were ecstatic, but little did we know the work we were about to put in. We graduated mid-May, but we still had to take and pass the NCLEX, because that was what made you an actual nurse, and it was required in order to continue with the bridge program. This bridge program literally started for us two weeks after we graduated. On top of that, we were scheduled to take our national exam after the new program had already begun. I remember I had to attend class the same day as taking my exam at a random time, something like 4:00 p.m. That's not ideal, if you ask me. Stress levels were off the charts. But I made it through the day and took the exam that could potentially have a crazy amount of questions, like over 275. Talk about another stress level, because you are staring into a computer screen that looks like it came out of the Stone Age. There was no back button, only "next." So you had no idea how many more questions were still ahead until the computer just shut off—a.k.a. the screen of death!

It was a minimum of seventy-five questions, which clearly sounded better than 275. So when my computer shut off, I just said, "Thank God," and left, praying I passed because I knew I would be dropped from the bridge program if I didn't. Forty-eight long hours later, I found out I passed the NCLEX! I felt a huge weight lift off of my shoulders, but there still was so much to do in the three semesters that were left. Just a few days later came a medication calculation test that required a 100 percent to pass; this was once again more stress, because limited attempts were given. Passing that was another huge relief that summer. I was beyond ready for that bridge program to end; I hated all of the exams. I stopped working as a CMA at this time and began working as a LPN. Work was now even more stressful because I was a new nurse.

Working in a skilled nursing facility setting was not for me. I was constantly bombarded by patients demanding pain medicine or unhappy family members demanding their family member be seen first. Meanwhile, I was just trying to find all of the medications in this heavy and unorganized medication cart that I had to wheel around while trying to simultaneously find my patients. Maybe they were in therapy or eating in the cafeteria or just in their room, which was not conveniently anywhere near my med cart. I decided that was not where I was going to learn anything at the pace that I needed, so I decided to work in a memory care unit. And let me tell you, I absolutely loved working with that set of individuals. Working with demented adults is very similar to working with toddlers. Every day is different. You never know what you will walk into or who is going to be unhappy. But I loved being able to engage in exercise classes with them.

The next semester was my final fall semester. I always liked the fall because of the seasons that change in the Midwest. I tried to spend as much time as I could outdoors, even if that included studying. But let's be honest, Starbucks or the library and designated study rooms got most of my attention because they had outlets where I could charge my laptop.

One of my nursing professors, who was also my assigned adviser, asked me some basic questions about my personal life. I remember telling her the truth. I was a single mom working multiple jobs while in school. She highly advised me to drop my jobs and focus on school. I told her I couldn't; that just wasn't an option for me, and I had made it through the LPN program doing the exact same thing.

Now I will say the RN program required so much more than the LPN in terms of time on campus and studying. So I decided to work Baylor option, where you can work two days and be paid for three. I worked as an LPN every single weekend 7:00 a.m. to 7:00 p.m. But the catch was I would get paid for thirty-six hours even though I only worked twenty-four hours. It just so happened they had to be weekends, which worked with my school schedule anyway. This still was not enough money, so I decided to take out two small student loans to help offset my living costs. Every single day for two semesters, I lived and breathed nursing, whether it was through school or working as a LPN.

I had no idea of the mental toll this was taking on me. Aside from being a mom, I was also in a relationship with someone I resided with. We didn't even really get along. We didn't have a lot of shared interests to begin with. I started to notice we fought more when I was under higher amounts of stress; it didn't change the fact that we would have been fighting about whatever it was at that time. But I noticed stress just added to it, and mind you, he took on a job change while I was doing my prerequisites, which was stressful for him as well. Plus, we moved into various housing arrangements during those five years.

One of those moves included moving into a home that one of his family members owned. We lived there with my boyfriend's father. This added so much unnecessary drama and stress that I truly wish I had never endured. However, it plays into my perspective based on *my experiences*. I already knew that my boyfriend was controlling, but I finally saw where he learned some of these behaviors. His father eventually apologized to me for his own actions, because *he was in the wrong.* And it's not that I was always in the right; he went to great lengths to attempt to control me. I believe he was this way because either he learned these controlling tactics from a previous generation, or he never learned how to appropriately handle his emotions. Therefore it showed up in these behaviors that affected me. The father was well into his sixties when we resided together, and I was barely 23 years old. He was a white older man, and I am biracial. It is important to keep those facts in the back of your mind as I continue on. I was the only female who lived in the house, so I automatically felt like my voice was almost never fully heard nor valued. At the time, I didn't have a ton of money so my boyfriend agreed to pay for a washer and dryer set with the expectation that I would do his laundry. This was a mutual agreement that seemed fair to me at the time. Laundry doesn't really bother me of all of the household duties. So I had my own laundry to do, plus my four-year-old son and now his laundry as well. As you can imagine, there was always laundry to do for three people. I needed to wash my scrubs because I only had two pairs of scrubs for work at the time. I couldn't stick to a set schedule for laundry for that purpose. If I worked three nights in a row, I had to do laundry; otherwise I wouldn't have had clean scrubs. Well this became a problem for my boyfriend's dad. He didn't like that I did laundry whenever I wanted to or had time to. He made sure it became a household rule that I had only a few set days a week to do laundry. I knew this was not even reasonable because I did a majority of the laundry in the house and I needed the washer and dryer available for my scrubs.

One morning I decided to start a load on "his" laundry day because he wasn't awake yet. I figured I would have some time to do it, and if he woke up it would already be in the dryer. This was the day that complete chaos broke out. When he found out I used the washer which was still mid-cycle at this point, he decided to stop it. He proceeded to throw all of my sopping wet clothes out of the washer onto the floor! They were so heavy because they were soaked and now the floor was a wet mess. This was on top of the fact that I had to rewash the entire load.

We did not get along prior to that morning, and it certainly became worse from there on. My son even remembers the events that happened next because he was there with me that morning. This is why I am so adamant that how a man treats a woman is important, especially in front of children who are watching. My boyfriend's father took my car keys off of the counter so I could not leave the house. He was approximately six feet tall, most definitely taller than me. He was dangling my keys with his arm in the air so I could not reach them as I was jumping up to reach for my keys and telling him to give them back. He did not pay my car note, so he had zero business in taking my car keys. I had to call a family member of theirs to intervene in order for me to get my keys back because I didn't want to get police involved. But unfortunately police became involved at a later date. After that washer incident, I knew I did not want to live with him anymore. I told my boyfriend I did not care if he decided to come with me, but I was not going to continue living there anymore with him. I was already stressed out at school; I didn't need to come home to more unnecessary stress.

Once I found an apartment, my boyfriend and I started the move-out process. However, I was not able to move all of my belongings in one fell swoop. One morning I had decided to go back to the house just a few days after the big furniture had been moved out. I realized my laptop was still there and I needed it for school. My boyfriend's dad was planning on moving out, but he was still going to reside there for a couple more weeks. I attempted to get in the door and quickly found out that his dad was going to put up a fight. He put all of his weight on the door so I could not push the door past him. I told him I was just there to get a few belongings and then I would be on my way out of there. He refused to open that door. He kept saying, "You don't live here anymore," and therefore I wasn't allowed in. I needed my laptop. I cannot tell you how seriously I took school at this point because I knew school was my *only* saving grace out of any situation in life I had been dealt. So I decided to call the cops because I knew I was not legally in the wrong. The cops showed up and I explained the situation. This didn't look good at all for an older white male not allowing a younger biracial female in the house.

The cops asked him and me how long we had resided there. The cops were perplexed by the tantrum this man was throwing, knowing I had actually moved into the property several weeks prior to him. The cops argued with him for approximately 30 minutes before he ultimately was forced to open the door to let me in. Legally he had no ground to stand on to keep me from entering the property, as I still had residency rights. I quickly grabbed my laptop and anything that I knew I needed, because I did not want to come back by myself again. We all ended up moving out of that house, but my boyfriend and I kept moving. Moving multiple times while in school, regardless of the reason for the move, only added to the stress of our extremely rocky relationship. And the fact that his immediate male family members did not like me only added to the situation.

At one point during our relationship one of my family members moved in related to a mental health crisis. I found myself alone in an unsafe situation as a young woman while I was driving my male family member to the hospital to get help. At the time he was having a full blown manic episode, and it pertained to how he was feeling about women at that moment in time. The entire car ride to the hospital was a horrifying experience for me. His manic episode was expressing what he wanted to do to all of the women in his life, which meant my life was in danger. I thought because I had worked with mental patients I was prepared for this. I thought I could truly help him, as I was one of the select few he trusted. I am so incredibly thankful that I was able to get him the help he desperately needed, but it cost me something internally. I love him to pieces to this day; however, I now have a boundary I've had to set in place for my personal safety. I had to learn that my safety and concerns needed to always come first.

I don't know how moving my male family member in affected my relationship with my boyfriend; I don't think it helped. But I know how it affected me during that time. Our relationship had a lot of different factors that weighed heavily on each one of us throughout the years we were together. I don't think there would have ever been a time where this recipe would have set us up for success. So I do extend grace to both him and myself in that manner. But the stress levels only rose, because now it was the end of my final semester, and then we left for Christmas break. Anyone remember COVID-19? This was the very end of 2019 when COVID was starting to be all over the news. We returned that January and had no idea how hard this was about to hit the health care system as well as any nursing programs during this time. I'm sure nobody really saw what was coming next.

One day we were in class, and the next day, everything moved online. Imagine having to attend your simulation lab where your patient is now your pillow that you have to perform CPR on. Imagine trying to keep a straight face as you use your pencil to apply ventilation to said pillow patient. Imagine classes now being on Zoom, and they required seeing your face in order to count for attendance. COVID aside, this was the hardest semester in terms of content. It was about emergency medication, code blues—the whole freaking nine. And maybe this is why I feel the way I do about emergency situations even to this day. It's correlated with an uneasy feeling because my last semester was ripped to shreds. We still had exams. Clinicals were eliminated. We somehow had to manage learning completely online without any hesitation. If you were a nursing student during this time, just know I stand with you in silence, because I know how much I was affected by this. But even this was nothing compared to what came next.

We graduated, and by that I mean no one had a ceremony to attend. We did not walk across a stage. I guess I could be glad I had been pinned at my LPN ceremony the year before. So I at least had an actual college graduation at this point. I still had to take NCLEX again, this time to be a RN. It had the same test structure but obviously different questions. I passed NCLEX, and then I received my graduation video. I remember laughing because this seemed so backward. But it was time to start my job, right in the middle of the pandemic. Talk about even more stress, because now I was taking care of actual COVID-19 patients.

Being a new grad nurse is hard in general. You feel like you want to ask a thousand questions, and so you ask the first one, realizing there's not enough time to ask the rest. On the floor I started on, orientation was supposed to be about six weeks long. Floors all across different health systems in our country became notorious for cutting new grads' orientations short by one or even two weeks due to short staffing needs. So imagine being a new nurse, knowing you need more time, and maybe even asking for more orientation time but being denied because there's already an entire patient load ready for you to take over. Oh, but wait, imagine working through that for a few months to only then be stretched to an unsafe nurse-to-patient ratio, and all of your patients are on extremely high volumes of oxygen, just trying to survive. Imagine sending emails to the higher-ups in administration but staffing ratios hardly change, if at all. Imagine even after all of the months and years after COVID-19 struck, the now unsafe patient ratio was expected and implemented as an *actual* ratio that occurs when we hit high volumes, which was now all of the time.

Imagine being that nurse. That's called burnout. That is why so many nurses left the field, which then created a huge shift to relying on travel nurses to come help. It was everywhere all across the United States and other countries too, I am sure. This was not an easy time to be a healthcare professional; there was no dollar amount that justified the things we saw and were forced to deal with. That was a mental toll I wasn't even remotely ready for after I felt like I barely survived nursing school.

I was stressed at work, school, and home. And school wasn't even eliminated at this point because I had to still go back to get my bachelor's! I had planned on doing the rest online; I chose to finish at Western Governor's University because of the price. I wasn't sure how much more I would receive in financial aid or if scholarships would continue. I was enrolled to start that following September, just a few short months after I graduated. But I knew if I wanted to actually finish, it was better for me to keep going and not take any time off.

It just so happened that my lease with my boyfriend was ending, and our relationship was shot by this point. I knew I had to leave for many reasons. Even if those last five years had been smooth sailing for me—all bills paid and completely eliminated childcare worries—we still would have not worked out. But none of those were the case anyway. I didn't know how bad a controlling relationship I had entered into until I was fully immersed in it. I was told I couldn't like the Kansas City Chiefs or Kim Kardashian because of how he felt about them. These were minor in comparison to the things he attempted to control me with. I was blamed for the unhealthy food we ate that caused him to gain weight. And as I look back, yeah, we both ate unhealthy food. I was accustomed to working in a lot of restaurants, so I was always around food, and my schedule was hectic. I did not spend time prepping meals back then. But even with that being said, I still made my own choices to not partake in food I didn't want to eat and that I knew was unhealthy for me. Just as I had a choice and a say in the matter, so did he. You cannot possibly blame me for *all* of the unhealthy habits that were formed when I was there.

However, there was no going back now to completely avoid a bunch of life lessons that came my way from those five years of torment. I clearly needed help. As my story unfolds, anyone can see that, feel that, and, even more importantly, understand that. But unfortunately, all of the help I began to receive was then completely weaponized against me behind closed doors. I stayed behind those closed doors for far too long because of all the self-doubt he instilled in me. I once truly believed I couldn't make it without him because of all of the help I needed that he made sure to remind me of *every* single time I attempted to leave. However, three years after I walked away from that relationship, I learned to heal and grow tremendously from that. Eventually I was able to heal even more from the previous relationship I had with my child's father. I gained a much healthier perspective and even became a better person because of it, so for that, I am extremely grateful today.

Chapter 4: Moving Forward
Learning to Love Myself

I found a new apartment for my son and me in October 2020, shortly after my bachelor's program began. My son's previous school year had also transitioned to online, and I quickly realized I was not made to be a teacher. Hats off to those special people who do this every day. I really do appreciate y'all. With a new apartment came a new school district. This was the most ideal change that could present itself. We quite literally upgraded school districts, and I immediately saw a huge change in his academics alone—and it was no longer online for him. When we first moved, it was hard. I was working night shift because I had to. I was the only parent who provided transportation to and from school. So night shift it was. But it did help me learn at a slower pace as a nurse compared to day shift. While it was necessary at the time, night shift was hard on me in more ways than one. I didn't really realize how much night shift alone affected me until a few years later.

My son and I got through that school year together. I also had to graduate from my nurse residency program, which took more time away from me. It always occurred once a month during day shift hours, and for some reason, our scheduler at work would always schedule new grads the night before residency and the night of. So I would get off work, go straight to residency from 8:00 a.m. to noon. Then I'd go back home to sleep for a few hours before going back to work. Can anyone say exhaustion? The unit I was on consisted of a bunch of friends who were all buddy-buddy with the scheduler and made sure they all had linked up schedules, which meant new grads got what was left, for the most part. Luckily, that was over in approximately ten months or so because I was well over that. At one point, our unit became short-staffed. Most of our experienced nurses left. I was now not considered a new grad because it was new grad season once again. At this point, I wanted to try some other avenue of nursing, so home health it was! But I didn't love it, and the way this company structured their pay meant if the patient didn't answer their door, you didn't get paid. You would think it wouldn't be that hard to track a patient down in a facility or show up at their house on an expected scheduled visit. That was not always the case, and I had enough of that. Fortunately, I had kept my job at the hospital, but I was only working as needed again.

I barely had a year and a half under my belt when I was asked to apply for the charge nurse position. I quickly realized this job position did not even remotely bring me joy. So I got a few months of experience and decided I would try a whole new different type of nursing. I never thought I would be able to even consider travel nursing because I had a child to raise, but local travel was a hot market at the time thanks to COVID-19. I took my first contract and knew this was something I wanted to continue for as long as possible. It was a standard thirteen-week contract on a floor that quite challenged me, to be honest. I learned that travel nursing is rolled into general nursing, but yes, there are still specialties. However, if you were a telemetry nurse, this was the land of opportunities. That contract set me up for the next one, which I landed in Jacksonville, Florida. I was ecstatic to stay with my best friend for seven weeks. I brought my ten-year-old son with me, and we rented a car. I was still on night shift, but somehow they only scheduled me on weeknights for a large majority of that contract. So every weekend, we would go to the beach. He stayed with me for half of my contract, and he flew back on the plane by himself. This was his first flying solo experience, and it gave me chills to realize how fast time had flown. I could still remember him being under two years old and being able to fly for free sitting on my lap. And now here we were, flying home separately.

While I was on my contract out of state, I decided I was done renting at my apartment complex. I felt like it had served its purpose, and I wanted to be in a house. I knew I wasn't ready to buy a home in that exact moment, so I'd be renting. But I didn't rent alone this time. This is where my life really began to transform. I'll need to take you back in time for a moment for you to understand how this all blossomed right in front of my eyes.

On February 11, 2016, I received a random message from a girl on Facebook. This message changed my entire life—not in one single day, but over time. At the time, I had just gotten off shift from serving, and I was walking down the street to the parking garage. I read the message and immediately called my best friend to tell her. This message was from my half sister on my biological dad's side. We had never met, but little did I know she was the girl in the photo my biological father had shown me back in 2008.

Naturally, this was awkward at first. If I am being completely transparent, I didn't even want another sister. I had three younger half sisters and three older adopted sisters. And since I grew up with my best friend, she became my sister because we clicked so well, and we both grew up as an only child in the home. I felt I didn't need another one, let alone *want* another sister, to be honest. But as she opened up to me over time, I could tell how badly she wanted this relationship. We would message off and on and stay up to date on each other's lives thanks to Facebook. When it came time for my LPN graduation in 2019, I decided I would send her an invite. I knew it was a fifty-fifty chance of her even showing up, as we hadn't even met in person yet. At this time, she was pregnant with a boy, and her daughter was growing out of the toddler stage. Well, to my surprise, she actually showed up to my graduation!

If you know me, you know I love pictures. I am from the era before smartphones where you would actually keep a camera on you. I can even remember having a Polaroid camera from Walmart back in the early 2000s that I would take on vacations to take pictures. Then my mom would take them to Walmart to have the pictures developed. I have pictures of the Grand Canyon, palm trees in Arizona, and playing on the Laguna Beach in California. As technology evolved, I upgraded my old Polaroid camera to a nice new pink Canon camera in middle school. Now things are different; every smart phone has a high-tech built-in camera—this became a game changer.

After my pinning, the rest of my family got to meet her as well. It was a little nerve-wracking because I didn't know how everyone else was feeling. But it was my first college graduation, so of course I was going to take pictures with everybody! And just like that, I took a picture that included her in it. We didn't even know each other all that well. Hell, we didn't even really know ourselves yet. I was only twenty-five years old, which would have made her twenty-three then.

I was really busy the following year, bridging from LPN to RN, but we would touch base every now and again on Facebook. As you know, there was not another graduation for us to celebrate together, thanks to COVID-19. When I moved into my solo apartment toward the end of 2020, this opened an opportunity for us to get to know each other better. By that time, I was in my bachelor's program, which was completely online. That made it so much easier for me to work and make more time for family and friends. I remember the first time we actually hung out at my apartment; she brought her two kids. That was the day I officially met my niece and nephew!

Trying to explain all of this to our kids was just like the first episode of *Sister, Sister* when Tia and Tamera finally meet and vow to never be separated again! But this story gets even crazier. We grew up within fifty miles of one another and never knew it. She was raised primarily by her mom with the help of our dad. If she decides to eventually write or tell her own story, I'll let her fill in those unique details. But she had spent years trying to find me on social media—and here is the real kicker. My name is spelled with a *K*. She was spelling it with a *C* and was unsure of my last name. She used to talk about her long search for me with her high school principal. Turns out, that principal was my very own high school volleyball coach!

The year 2021 was a year full of love, fun, and travel. That's the year I really formed a tight sisterhood between myself, my only half sister on my dad's side (whose name is Reyna), and my second oldest half sister on my mom's side (whose name is Mariah). We are all within five years of age, we're biracial, we're single moms, and we've shared some bloodline traumas and desired to break generational curses together. The three of us eventually went on to get a matching sister tattoo that represented our sisterhood. Our bond is rare and unique—something I am grateful for today.

It's also the year I met my biological dad for the second time. But a few things had changed. Now remember, I had only seen this man the one time in 2008. I just did the math—that was literally thirteen summers prior, the exact same age I lost the father who raised me! *Wow*, I am telling you right now, only God can take credit for all of the miracles that have happened in my life. I spent thirteen years with a father and thirteen years without one. To now having a renewed opportunity for a father-daughter bond. God had plans I didn't understand and couldn't really see in the moment. We lost touch not because he wanted to but because of some family drama that interfered. I have no hard feelings to this day. I don't hold it against anyone, because no one could stop what God had planned for us.

My biological father's health had declined by this point. Thirteen years was pretty significant for him. He was now a dialysis patient three days a week, and he had diabetes with multiple complications that included glaucoma and a prosthetic left leg. It was hard to process, that I knew our relationship would be limited. He couldn't drive, couldn't see very well, and couldn't walk long distances. That limits a lot of dreams for a daughter. I never thought we could have something as simple as sharing a vacation together. But I honestly can't imagine what that was like for him. I had recently turned twenty-seven. We had already missed a lot of the big milestones to celebrate over the years together. But honestly, so had my sister Reyna. While she was able to spend a lot more time with him in comparison to me at this point, her memories with him were still limited. Our dad lived a very interesting life, and we both can honestly say we only know a handful of pieces to his puzzle. His memory is not that great, but he still manages to know the streets of Kansas City so well, even as a legally blind man. His English is broken, and his accent only adds to it when you try to hold a conversation with him. But my sister and I really bonded over this as time went by.

Another thing Reyna and I had in common was that our birth moms were white and struggled with addiction. Hers just happened to still be living. Our biological dad has very dark skin, as he is Cuban. Because we are biracial, our skin complexions are similar, and we both have the ability to tan easily. But the texture of our hair is vastly different. These similarities and differences eventually grew our relationship even more.

In 2021, we spent the summer mostly poolside at my apartment or at Oceans of Fun. We even went on our first vacation with our kids! We took them on a train (a first for us all) to St. Louis. We stayed in a really ratchet Airbnb that looked like it belonged on an episode of *Shameless*. We wanted to keep this trip cheap, so we decided not to get a rental car—huge mistake. Instead, we used Ubers to get everywhere. This might sound great until you have to fold up a heavy stroller, forget to bring a car seat, or have to convince the driver to let one of the adults sit in the passenger seat in her standard four-door car because there was a total of five of us to haul away. That was a super fun trip—forty-five minutes back to the Airbnb after spending a whole day sweating with the kids at Six Flags! But the one thing I can say about my sister and me is that we go to extremely great lengths to show up for our kids. And when we do it together, it's always like watching magic happen!

Before we knew it, most of the year had gone by, and it was now time for the holidays. Reyna had told our brother that she had finally found me and formed this relationship. He ended up reaching out, and I got to know him a little bit as well. I even invited him over for Thanksgiving! That is the day I officially met my half brother and his son. Here goes another nephew! Between all of my half siblings, I now had four nephews and only one niece! That was a special holiday that year for me.

Now for 2022, the most eventful and exciting year of my entire adulthood! I experienced a lot of personal growth and development after reading books like *The New Single* by Tamsen Fadal that year. It brought me a lot of perspective, which came from a respectable middle-aged woman who provided some solid personal advice at a time when I felt I could relate. I discovered later that this was when I embarked on the journey through learning to truly love myself and find myself in womanhood. This was also the year that really brought Reyna and me closer, together with our dad. I started my first local contract that year, which led me to my out-of-state contract. While I was out of town, Reyna came to visit me one weekend. We spent the most fabulous weekend on the beach and explored local restaurants. She somehow convinced our friend and me to eat at a Cuban restaurant. We had so many leftovers that I gave a plate full of food to a homeless man who was pushing a shopping cart in an empty parking lot. They thought I was crazy for getting out of the car to flag this man down. They also hysterically laughed over the fact that I got hit on by the homeless guy as I was wearing my high-waisted light wash blue jean shorts.

I never wanted our laughter to end, which is why I was so excited to ask her if she wanted to get a place together when my contract was done. Before I knew it, we'd secured a deposit on a rental house and were preparing to move in with our kids early that fall. September came, and it was move-in time! Our dad's health was declining, and so the plan was to move him to a facility for the time being. He was renting to own a property that he was currently sub-leasing to a terrible tenant. Reyna had moved him into her place temporarily, but his health decline required more than she could handle by herself. Our dad ended up moving in with us, which was not the original plan. But I couldn't be more grateful and thankful for the memories that were created during this lease.

While we were moving into the rental house, I was finishing up my last few courses for my BSN. With my university being online, that meant every month or so, a graduation ceremony was held in a different state. I had done my research and looked at the timeline several months prior and told myself I wanted to be able to make the ceremony in Orlando, Florida. It was being hosted in mid-November 2022, which meant I had to have all of my courses submitted and passed the month prior in order to walk. In order to meet that deadline, I had to really take things seriously despite 2022 being a really exciting year full of travel and experiences. I had to reserve a spot ahead of time for graduation, even though my classes weren't completely finished yet.

For those who don't know me, if I want it bad enough, I am going to work hard to make sure I get it. I received an email saying all of the spots were *full* for graduation. My heart sank! All of the work I had put in felt like it was swept out from underneath me. While I was devastated, I still prayed for a different outcome and continued finishing my courses on the timeline, just in case.

Like the fourth quarter of dang near every Chiefs' game, things turned around for the better, and it was a win for Kansas City—but this time, it was a win for Kristina! I received an email saying my spot was now secured, and just like that, it was official. I was graduating with my bachelor's degree—the first female in the family to bring home that trophy!

Remember I said that this out-of-town ceremony took a lot of planning? I wasn't lying. I had planned for a year for my family to come down, and we would all rent an Airbnb for the celebration. I'm talking like twelve family members from Kansas City. We planned on taking the kids to Disney World as well. We were going to be in Orlando, so we had to—duh! Well, a good half of my family backed out just a few months before graduation. I remember feeling really disappointed. I tried to give everyone adequate time to have their finances in order to be able to make this happen. This was such a big deal to me. This was the last graduation of my lifetime, but more importantly, I went through literal hell and back to achieve it. I just wanted to celebrate that with the ones I had spent limited amounts of time over the course of those six years that it took for me to wrap this journey up to begin with. That's all.

Reyna went to great extremes to really come through for me. She knew how much emotion was poured into this journey and how much my heart ached that my parents would never see me walk on any of the stages. Reyna drove down with her kids, and she managed to get our dad on a plane. And I just want to stop there for a second to acknowledge how much of a highlight of a trip this was for him. Our dad had not been on a plane in over *forty years*. He was only on this mini-vacation for forty-eight hours, and it must have been a wild time for him. Yet not once did he complain. He lost his phone somehow before the plane took off, and even worse, he left his walker at the freaking KCI airport. And to keep this momentum going, his flight that was already landing extremely late got delayed. So he ended up arriving at 4:00 a.m. on the day of my graduation, but remember, he didn't have a phone to call anyone. Reyna had planned on picking him up at the Orlando airport at his expected arrival time, only to find out his plane was still in the air for several more hours, which is how this came to be a 4:00 a.m. adventure. This man flew disabled with a prosthetic leg, missed a day of dialysis in order to fly out the day prior, had poor vision, and lost the only phone he had to communicate with us, and *still* managed to not miss this event to see his first-born walk across that stage.

We managed to make it to Disney World, which was the first time for my sister and her two kids. My best friend and her mom drove down from Jacksonville to meet us in Orlando for the ceremony. My cousin also drove down with his daughter from Kansas City. And that was the best ceremony experience; Daymond John from *Shark Tank* was a guest speaker! His speech was incredibly moving; he is a phenomenal public speaker, I might add. My best friend told me that my biological dad's eyes lit up when I walked across that stage. I am so eternally grateful for the all of the effort Reyna put into this trip to pull that off. I know I've told her thank you countless times, but I say it again from the bottom of my heart. Not even just for me, but for our dad too.

We had a delicious celebratory dinner after, and of course, there were many pictures taken that day. We young adults hit up downtown Orlando that evening; the 10:00 p.m. traffic was not worth it, by the way. The next day, we took the kids to the beach. This was my niece's and nephews' first beach experience. Just like their mom and aunt, they fell in love with it. But all vacations eventually come to an end, so we went back home.

My sister and I knew this lease wasn't going to be long-term. I began thinking about what I wanted to do next. My upbringing left me with the idea that I was going to be married before I bought a house. To even take that a step further, my last relationship really drilled into my head that I wouldn't be able to buy a home on my own. Remember how he told me that I couldn't afford my car insurance without him? Well, I could, and it was actually cheaper being on my own policy! So I decided to put in a mortgage application just to see what would come of it. I really wasn't expecting to buy a home in that moment. But I was shocked to see how much they were willing to loan me! That was one of the happiest moments of my life, knowing all of the ups and downs it took to get there.

Then the search began. I knew hardly anything about the house buying process. It's a bumpy, drawn-out process if you ask me. I had no idea it would remind me of the ups and downs that my nursing journey gave me. When I was growing up, society made it seem like buying a home was just as simple as saying, "I bought my first house!" Boy, was I wrong. I really didn't even tell many family members that I was going to buy a home until I had already put money down in escrow. I didn't want to be talked out of it just because interest rates were high, or they thought I should wait until marriage, or whatever—the list could go on and on. To surprise everyone even more, I bought a house in a city I had zero experiences in. But for me, this was a great reminder that this was a fresh start, a blank canvas that I could fill with any new happy and healthy memories that I wanted to. I didn't realize how close it actually ended up being to the other cities I was more familiar with, but this change was a good one for me. I had to change some habits because I was no longer conveniently located near any food chains. So this forced me to learn how to really cook at home. I bought a new build in an area that was in the early stages of development. This has turned out to be a great real estate investment,—something I can pass on to my child when he comes of age. By then, this area will look vastly different as more and more new builds continue to go up. But it took some time for me to come across this particular house.

The first new build I checked out just did not sit right with me. The woman who showed me the property came off like she would be doing me a favor to sell me this house. It did not have any super attractive features for the price point it was listed at, for one. But I realized that was on purpose because they made more money on the upgrading of those missing features. She told me, "Oh, you're a single mom! We can cut you a discount to upgrade to the flooring and black matte finishes that you like." I didn't need her to cut me any discount just for the simple fact that I was a single mom buying a home by myself. But thanks for the offer, along with the hefty escrow payment she was asking from me to hold this cookie-cutter container-looking home.

So the search continued. I ended up finding a much cuter home and better deal from a more level-headed builder, thanks to my wonderful real estate agent. She got my escrow down to less than half of what the previous builder was asking. From the moment I stepped into this home, I knew instantly *that this was the one* for me. It even had the black matte finishes without any upgraded price! I later got to decorate this house with how I felt about living on my own. I even went on to buy a crystal chandelier that represented my style and who I had become. I absolutely loved working with a woman who had experience of closing on new builds, because little did I know how stressful this was going to be.

Closing on a new build was even crazier than I imagined. Talk about builder timelines coming down to the very last freaking minute so the property can close on time. But we did it. I closed on my very first home in the summer of 2023 at the age of twenty-nine and as a biracial single mom *without* a cosigner or a man's name next to mine. I also became the youngest homeowner on the block (who also happened to be the *only* biracial one), but I've never been afraid of standing out. Because I have always stood out my entire life.

Chapter 5: Adoption and Culture
Love the Skin You're In

My half sisters and I were the only biracial people *period* at family reunions growing up. And I am not going to lie here; I felt uncomfortable most times. These family reunions would typically have thirty to fifty people there, and everyone was completely white but me. I just didn't know how to express that, nor did I know how to navigate my feelings about it. So I was always quiet. The family I grew up in did great at loving me and raising me in certain ways. But they did me absolutely zero justice in this department. You couldn't love my curls without also loving the other half of my bloodline. You couldn't appreciate my big brown eyes without also appreciating the culture behind them. You couldn't see my skin color but not see I would be missing out on the race and ethnicity that made it that way. When you say, "We don't see color," this is the exact problem that is created. And this is not a personal attack on any of my white family members. I just want you to understand how I felt.

As I have grown into this adult body, I realized how much I had to learn to love my hair, appreciate my skin color, and accept that I am not cultured at all, largely because of my upbringing. I wore my hair straight in middle school. Why? Because that's all I ever saw growing up. I was tired of being called a poodle because of my thick mixed hair. No one educated me on hair products for mixed girls. No one taught me how to do edges. No one showed me treatments that were good for my kind of hair. My mom used to put Paul Mitchell products in my hair to show off my bouncy curls when my hair was long, and that was fine for the time being. But there is a reason why Paul Mitchell hair products aren't in the ethnic hair product section at any store. And I never had been in a mixed hair section of any store or salon until I was an adult. So growing up, it was either my hair was a mess or it was straight—and that only lasts so long. Humidity affects my hair tremendously, and greasy hair didn't help maintain it either.

I had my hair braided one time during my entire childhood, and I can bet anyone who is not white can see where this is going. Because it is a trendy concept for any woman of any color to get it done while on vacation, mine just happened to be in the Bahamas. That was my only real personal experience with braids as a child around the age of five. Now imagine that. The only time I truly saw braids on a consistent basis was at my predominantly African American school. This school is the only reason I have any cultural identity outside of knowing a completely straight and narrow Christian life. I never listened to the radio until I was in middle school; that's when I began testing household limits.

My best friend has a memory of me, and it's not a pleasant one. I was upset that my parents had bought me yet again another Christian CD, and I was in middle school at this point. I knew what else was out there, and so I let my mom know I was pissed. But can you really blame me as you start to understand my upbringing? Back then, I didn't even know how to articulate what I can say about it now, so it came off as being pissed, entitled, and borderline bratty. And those emotions continued even through young adulthood.

We didn't have social media access when I was growing up like we do now. My parents didn't allow me on YouTube when we finally had more than just dial-up Internet. I'm from that era when you couldn't be on the home phone (which was attached to the wall, you Gen Z kids) at the same time as the Internet. Just think about a child who never saw a powerful biracial role model, not someone in the media, and certainly not in her immediate life. Think about how that might affect someone when they learn their truth. It's a lot to process and untangle.

And what kind of music did my parents listen to? White artists. I was groomed and conditioned to be in church and to be uncultured without even really knowing it. As a child, I never listened to top hits unless it was a Christian artist—who was always white, might I add. No wonder I always wanted to have blond hair and blue eyes, two things that were never going to ever happen to me. But I was made to love myself because I was made in God's image, so why didn't I have role models in my life to look up to that even remotely looked like me? Was that because I was allowed to play with American Girl dolls to represent someone like me, as if that was enough? When I was adopted, that whole ethnic side was completely wiped clean. My family may not even understand this chapter and may have to reread it. But I am going to speak up on this one, loud and proud.

I never even knew how suppressed this was for me until full-blown adulthood. When I used to be a server, I would always meet new people each day. They would usually ask me the same question: "Where are you from?" And this never bothered me. I didn't think much of it when I was eighteen to twenty-four years of age even though, internally, I felt to the core how uncultured I was. I was a little busy trying to survive back then. But as the years went on and I took courses like psychology, I started to notice some things. Now instead of serving tables, I was taking care of patients. And the questions only dug deeper.

"Do you speak Spanish?"

"How long have you lived here?"

"Did you grow up here?"

And when Reyna and I really started getting into some deeper, more vulnerable topics like this, I quickly realized how I truly felt deep down inside. We shared the same feelings for similar reasons because we grew up in white families. I found that this was more common than I even realized growing up mixed. Her daughter, who is my niece, was now having these same internal struggles. This is where I found my strength again in womanhood and through the culture we all shared. It is a constant learning experience for all of us, but we knew the importance of educating her early on to know why her skin and hair should be embraced *and* celebrated.

When my biological father shared a particular photo with me in 2021, it sparked so many questions. I met this man for the very first time to my knowledge when I was fourteen years old. How did he have this picture of him holding me as a *newborn*? And why is that the *only* photo we had together? I remember thinking, "Am I sure that isn't my sister Reyna?" But it wasn't. It was, in fact, me because I recognized the carpet in the kitchen at my parents' house, the one I grew up in. I only vaguely remember the thin dark pattern carpet, but it is in many of my baby photos that are stored away.

He always used to wear suits and apparently very flashy rings as this picture shows. But he looked so proud to be a first-time father in this photo. So what happened? This is where his story meets mine, and as I heard him talk about it, my heart broke for him. He made his own choices back in his home country in Cuba that made him no longer welcome by the Cuban government, so he ended up in the States. He couldn't go back even if he wanted to. He left behind his parents and siblings, and he unfortunately never saw them again. He somehow got involved with my biological mom, and when it was made clear that I was being adopted, my parents came off as threatening to him. So as someone who feared of being thrown back in jail, he stayed far away from me when my parents told him he wasn't welcome to come around. He felt that as a person of color, he was inferior to them, and it hurts my heart to this day that is his how he perceived the situation. It is incredibly hard for me to think that my parents would have threatened him, but I know first-hand how far they were willing to go to protect me from the outside world. But nonetheless, no matter what was said or done, no matter what someone's perception or reality was, the outcome was still devastating for him and for me, even years later.

As a biracial person, it just doesn't sit well at all. Adoption and safety concerns aside, what about culture? This was literally the other half of me! Even more important-ly, what about his desire to be some kind of father to me? What if the opportunity would have made him become an even better one? I could have had relationships with my oth-er two half siblings growing up. We will never know, because that was simply just decided for me. I was very well protect-ed on the outside from my adoption, but on the inside, I was always torn apart. And it unfortunately just validates how culture was knowingly taken away from me and never even incorporated or attempted for me to learn. I never grew up with books about Cuba or even how to make Cuban food. I was only taught how to read and write in English as a child, but why never Spanish too? Nobody thought I would ever want to know about my Cuban aunts or uncles or cousins?

On my twenty-eighth birthday, my biological dad made me a piñata. It's something that might be so simple to the rest of the world, but it meant so much to me. It was like I was able to give him back just one of my childhood birthdays to celebrate with him. He put candy and money in there, which was funny because my son and his cousins were all fighting for what fell out of it. But the feeling of trying to give back lost time to someone is a harsh reminder that you can't go back in time.

I would have never chosen to structure the way my adoption went. To complicate things further, I was the first and the only one who was adopted by my great-grandparents. This was because they also once raised my biological mom (who was their grandchild) up until a certain point in childhood. There were a lot of things going on back then that I can't really speak to because I wasn't conceived yet, but I do know it broke their hearts when she left their home. So when they found out that my biological mom was pregnant with me, they didn't want me to go through the struggles they saw firsthand with their own grandchild. I am not sure if they thought she would go on to have more kids, which she did a few years later. Maybe my parents didn't want to raise any more kids, as I was already the fifth one in their lifetime. Subsequently, my grandma adopted and raised my other three half sisters that my biological mom had. As I was growing up, there was always tension between every female in my family, from great-grandma to grandma to biological mom, all the way down to between me and my half sisters. The adults were unhappy with how the adoptions were split up, as if this should have been a war to begin with. And then because I grew up with a very much different upbringing than my three younger half sisters, I practically had the silver spoon in my mouth growing up. Yet none of us kids asked to be split up. None of us kids asked to live completely different social and economic lives that would go on to affect our perspectives of life and choices as time went on.

I knew I would never want adoption for my child because of the heartaches I experienced, and so I kept mine. People tend to think it was a beautiful thing that I was raised in my family and not just adopted into a stranger's hands. To some degree, they were right. But it caused a ton of continuous family drama for decades between the women. I didn't even fully understand all of its complexities then. My adoption had so many different variables to it: multiple races, multiple generations, addiction, adopted siblings, half siblings, and different cultures. And yet somehow, for the most part, it was stable. Isn't that wild? I truly feel that God put me on this earth to be able to show you that you can put so many differences aside and still find unity in one another. You just have to learn how to properly navigate natural emotions to come together to do that. I just wish everyone else saw that too.

Chapter 6: Parenting
Never Stop Apologizing

My son is now currently twelve years old and in the sixth grade. I noticed some behavior changes and knew something deeper was going on. But I wasn't thinking it had anything to do with his skin color, and there were other things that were bothering him too. But when he expressed how conflicted he felt trying to choose a race and ethnicity on an exam, I knew it was time for me to speak my truth. And in order for me to speak my truth, I had to have a clear understanding of myself. I didn't want him to figure out who he was in adulthood like I did. There should be an option to select "mixed" and leave it at that for children. If you came from a cultured family, that is wonderful, and I am genuinely happy for you. But if you didn't, you understand this unnecessary feeling that's given to you for no reason. It's a sense of belonging that gets taken from you. Could we learn Spanish today? Sure, but it doesn't make up for the rest of the culture we missed out on. This was just one of the many things I got to apologize to my son about.

My parents never really apologized to me growing up, but back then, I never really felt like I needed one from them. They weren't stressed after a long day. They were retired when they raised me. There was no waking up early or being pressed for time for them, even though they did wake up to watch the daily 6:00 a.m. news. I love to imagine every now and then a world in which I didn't have to always constantly be somewhere and needed so I could be more present with my own child—the type of parent that I had growing up.

Becoming a parent at seventeen years old meant I was in for it. I definitely wasn't grown the day I turned twenty years old. I did not have it figured out at all. I was never on time to anything once I got my own car. I was late to my own prom, and to this day, my friends still never let that one slide! Truly, I didn't even feel like I had a good idea of what life really entailed until my later twenties, and I certainly didn't know what I deserved until then as well. So with every season came a lesson and subsequently another reason for me to apologize as time went by. But that takes a lot of honesty and transparency within yourself to even admit fault to your innocent child. Children really do learn primarily by watching, not always listening. So I pray my actions over time will always outweigh my past verbal responses when I was exhausted and stressed while constantly remaining in survival mode. With this discovery of the power of apologizing came a hunger for deeper understanding. That deeper understanding led to an even bigger realization. I began to recognize the generational curses that ran in my family that absolutely had to be demolished. And that starts with recognition and accountability.

Chapter 7: Breaking Generational Curses
The Good, the Bad, and the Ugly

I saw generational curses in my family before I knew that was the term to call it. I just called them patterns. I watched three out of four of my older siblings live with our parents during my childhood. And the fourth one would have probably done it too, but she was left out of the will, so there wasn't a chance of her living in that house. My older brother moved in when I was in elementary school and resided there until the house was sold. My other two older sisters lived there while I was in high school and a little beyond. This meant they were all well in their middle-aged adulthood when they resided there. Each one had a different reason, but their reasons all tied back to their own personal choices and finances. I saw that was not normal when I looked at other families, but it was somehow just accepted in mine. And maybe they saw it as a blessing, but each one of their own adult children was now living with them—and their grand-kids. That is a generational curse at its finest, if you ask me.

I can't speak to everyone's situation, but when your own kids end up back in your house as middle-aged adults, history is repeating itself. Somewhere down the line, mistakes were made and never corrected. When the house I grew up in was sold, that unsettling feeling lit a fire under my ass. I was not going to live under someone else's roof for years or even decades to come like I saw growing up. Living on your own is not easy, but it's possible with self-discipline. If you always know you can go back somewhere when times get tough, it's easy to find yourself doing just that. But your perspective changes when you don't have that luxury, and so do your habits over time.

Another generational curse I realized early on was the destruction of sisterhood. Women are always stronger when they come together. The fact that the mom who raised me had a bad enough relationship with one of her daughters for her to leave her out of the will showed me that the women in my family needed repair. That same daughter did not have great relationships with her sisters or her own daughter, who was my biological mom. And because of that, I didn't have a great or close relationship with my biological mom or grandma. It's more than just the drugs and addictions. Hearts were clearly hurting long before the need to suppress those feelings with substances.

Women before us should be able to communicate effectively with one another to change that dynamic for the younger generations. And what I have come to realize over time is this line of women all had something missing in their own hearts. You can't possibly blame just one single person for every crack in numerous relationships that's passed down from one generation to the next. Sometimes you have to take some accountability too, especially if you want change.

There is so much truth to the statement that the right people for your soul see you differently. They hear you differently. And because of that, they show up, support, and nourish you differently. That is how your glass becomes overflowing so you can then pour into someone else who needs it. Those people are the ones who you choose to be a part of your community. I understand the need for healthy boundaries, as they are important. But there is a defined line between healthy boundaries and completely cutting somebody off. Repaired relationships can have healthy boundaries; it just takes time and some internal work to heal properly. Cutting someone off is not loving your neighbor as yourself, nor is it loving your enemy from a distance.

I saw and felt all of these cracks growing up. I was not nourished properly with the lack of womanhood or culture I desired to have. My adoption within the family only led to more hardened cracks between these women. Somehow, I was being protected from the outside world, yet I was feeling like I was being suffocated on the inside. Is this how I was supposed to treat other women? Because the Bible I studied while growing up did not guide women to treat each other like this. And I wasn't the only one who noticed this. My friends noticed. My generation of half sisters noticed, because we lived through it. My male cousins even noticed. Who you are as an adult will tell if you actually healed from your own traumas. So at what point does a heart finally get the healing it desperately needs? After it's too late at the gravesite?

Chapter 8: Womanhood
Man, I Feel Like a Woman

I knew deep down I didn't want to have a daughter first when I was pregnant, and lucky for me, I had a son. I lacked a traditional family tree where I had a close-knit relationship with my grandma. I felt like I didn't know enough about being a woman to really pass that knowledge down to another little girl, because it was never really passed down to me. It is by far more than just dressing in cute clothes with your hair done and some polish on your nails while you sit with your legs crossed and a smile on your face. Understanding what a woman was really about came in my later twenties. I have a very special memory of a time that my newfound sisterhood came together when one of us was hurting. The two of us came to the other's side without any hesitations and any judgments. We helped clean the inside of her apartment and came across a dress I had worn many years before. That dress became a part of the *Sistahood of the Traveling Dress* as it now traveled with the sister who stumbled upon it. In that moment, I realized how much of a leader I had become in my journey of womanhood, something that wouldn't have occurred the way it did if I had been in my previous relation-ship. I now had this large sense of freedom to really blossom into who I was meant to be.

I came from women who were from an era of being silenced, who didn't pass on to the next generation how to stand up for themselves. I do give grace to my older siblings because they were raised with the same parents who taught us the same principles. However, I *do not* stand with some of the responses they tend to give, whether it is just silence or asking, *What would Jesus do*? I have learned how to ex-press how I feel and talk to people in my community that truly know how to nourish and support one another, not just claim to listen. I've also learned how to acknowledge some-thing that isn't right and stand up for myself, even if that means I am standing alone. These older generations tend to stand with the phrase *let's not air our dirty laundry*. They also tend to look down on someone who chooses to speak up about their experiences, instead of standing with them. Considering my parents who raised me were six decades older than me, it is no wonder I was groomed to be that same way growing up. Eventually, I learned how to do that on my own, with a big thanks to my younger sisters. We have a special bond from the things that we share that make us unique, but I've learned how to celebrate our differences. Being a woman of color should be celebrated and protect-ed. *All women should be celebrated and heard everywhere,* as we have come a long way to get here. Women are no lon-ger backing down; instead, we are standing up. Therefore, the more we *stand together, the stronger we become*.

Having the opportunity to do travel nursing really opened my eyes as a single woman, especially when I trav-eled to a hospital I had never stepped foot in before. I got to meet so many incredible women from all over the world. And no matter where we came from, what we left behind, or what we were working so hard for, we all shared one thing in common. We showed up to support one another for our patients. The amount of strength it took some of these women who came from other countries to have two-year international contracts in an unfamiliar place showed me how strong women had truly become. I was just so proud to be in their presence after listening to their humbling stories.

I've learned that I particularly love hearing older women tell their own stories. Meeting elderly single women, whether that was by choice or by becoming a widow, opened my eyes to womanhood beyond the golden years. I've listened to their stories about how they overcame multiple hardships and still continue to progress. One woman in particular showed me that you can be as young as your body will allow you to be. There is no limit when you set your mind that you still want to do something. Being physically active daily can look differently for any woman, but you're not limited to only being able to lift two-pound dumbbells or only taking walks around the block. You can still run despite being nearly eighty years old; you just might not be as in a hurry to the finish line as you thought you'd be.

Another woman I had the pleasure of meeting while taking care of her told her family that she really appreciated having me in particular for her care. I, of course, said thank you, but I really thought about that statement and how much it meant to me. I listened to her story of selling her land and giant home after her husband recently passed. I wondered how she would take care of her new house, even though she had family nearby that would be more than willing to help. A house can be a lot of work, which is why she bought a new build. That is exactly what I did, and I thought to myself, *She's a smart woman too.*

Chapter 9: Faith, Forgiveness, and Friendships
May Your Faith Be Bigger than Your Fears

I grew up believing in God, but I realized my faith was not as strong as I thought it was. After my dad died in 2008, my church life died with it. I had tried to go back to that same church after the incident. My mom certainly did not stop going. But I just couldn't take it anymore as time went on. It was hard being in the same youth group with that same boy, knowing my dad was no longer here because of his actions. He had apologized so many times to me and my mom, but that didn't relieve any of the grief I was going through. And to even complicate this further, my family decided to file a lawsuit.

I understood why lawsuits matter. I understood what winning this lawsuit could do for my family. I even understood that we actually had a case. But was it worth it, even if we did win? Money is *not* everything, and it still does not matter to me as much as it does to even the average person. And what would happen if we did not win? Did anyone think about that? I was fifteen years old when this thing went to trial. There were countless depositions grooming me to take the stand. Do you know what taking the stand did to me? Do you know how hard it was for me to stand up there and face people I didn't even know to try to persuade them to be on our side instead of the church's? There should have never been a side to begin with; this was not a complete accident! I could barely say anything; I had tears streaming down my face and a pain so deep that when I talked, my throat hurt. I felt nauseous and clammy. I was only fifteen years old; this was not a setting I should have ever been in at this age. I should have been enjoying time with friends, learning more about myself, and thinking about what I wanted to do after I graduated high school. Instead I was stuck in a courthouse, trapped with people I didn't ever want to see again. And yet, it's just something I had to go through that caused me more pain and suffering.

The jury decided the church had no fault. So my family lost the lawsuit, and life went back to whatever it was. My mom eventually joined a new church. I think this lawsuit finally did her in. She begged me to attend with her, and I just could not get myself to do it. My faith was at its all-time low, and I just couldn't see how I could ever attend church again. It had become a part of my identity that was now completely ripped away from me. Church had always been my home away from home. This was a soul-breaking loss for me over the years. I struggled with cognitive dissonance with church and faith. However, while my previous fiery faith was dim, it was not completely extinguished.

When I was eighteen years old, I decided to get the word "faith" tattooed on the back of my neck. It was my reminder that while I can't always see it, it's always there with me. I needed that reminder to keep going. When my baby daddy and I first had our son, we argued about faith and religion. At the time, he was a Jehovah's Witness, and I had grown up in an Assemblies of God background. We clashed so hard in our beliefs, and eventually this didn't matter anymore because he no longer believed in his religion. While I still believed in mine, I was not committed to a church at this time. So looking back, what were we even arguing for?

Another important tattoo that I have is in memory of the one and only Miss Charlotte Reagan McCann, made with her very own ashes into a beautiful butterfly on the back of my left shoulder. Her sixty-eight days on earth moved so many people in different cities across the country, so much that her parents decided to start a business called Your Angel's Ink. They made a memorable and creative way for ashes to become tattoo ink as a permanent and physical part of your journey. Everywhere you go, you carry a part of them with you. Even as time goes on and you grow older, while they are no longer here, that tattoo will always remain.

After my mom died, I visited a small handful of churches during my young adulthood, but they never really felt like home to me. I was even invited to attend church with family or childhood friends I grew up with that I had known for twenty years at this point. I still never felt like I was in the right church for me. However, my best friend continued to encourage me to try again until I found the one. But even if I did find the one, my crazy work and school schedule never allowed me to consistently attend. COVID-19 changed a lot, especially in the church world. Now churches were streaming online; no virus could stop what God was doing behind the scenes.

I managed to come across some TikTok videos of a man named Pastor Mike Todd who was preaching about being cuffed to cash and control. Transformation Church became my new home that day. I loved that this pastor was not your average white man in a suit who seemingly never did wrong and had all of the answers all of the time. He was African American, and his congregation did not have only two African Americans like where I grew up. I loved that he was so blatantly honest and so transparent with his own testimony in his personal life. I wanted this role model for my son, and so after I had watched a few sermons for myself, we made this a tradition for the two of us. I was still working night shift at the time, but I always made sure every week, even if it wasn't Sunday, to watch these sermons. We even made a three-and-a-half-hour trip down to Tulsa, Oklahoma, to see him speak. He did not preach that day, but that was okay! But I knew in that moment this church was meant for me. I called my best friend to tell her I had finally found my home church, and she was really supportive of that. She knew firsthand how much this meant to me. My life was not only transformed, but it allowed my heart to heal as I continued to follow along online every week. I am not perfect by any means. But this church became a great reminder that we were meant to be human. We were meant to share our stories to help the generation that is under us and even above us! We were meant to make mistakes, but more importantly, we were meant to heal and come together in unity. That is where I wanted to be. That was where I was meant to be! So I began sharing his sermons with my sister Reyna. Eventually, I began sharing with other family members too. Now I am not sure how this affected them. But if you are reading and haven't felt that shift of heart yet, maybe reading this chapter will finally allow you to feel what I was trying to pour into your cup.

Chapter 10: Finances and Credit
Extreme Money Makeover

Growing up my mom always told me, "Kristina, save your money. Save it for a rainy day!" But she never really explained that, nor did she adequately prepare me for this lesson. I often wonder if both of my parents would have lived until I was at least twenty-five years old if I would have been better equipped. But by the time it came time to really talk heavy about finances, I was already adding to my plate by having a baby. There wasn't much time to prepare; nine months was nowhere near long enough to save up with what I had going on. And I did not start out on the right foot either. I knew almost nothing about the two major things that unfortunately make the world go round.

I just want to give a huge shoutout to my best friend and her mom in this chapter because they left such a lasting impression to start with. To me, they somehow got it right; I never watched my best friend struggle in the real world and then end up back at good ol' mom and dad's house. Maybe they weren't rich, but they were financially more literate than my family. Her mom told me to "save at least three to

six months of your expenses." And I still didn't really understand that concept at eighteen years old because what bills
did I really have back then? The only consistent bill I had was
a phone bill that seemed to get cut off because I didn't pay
it on time. I had rent in various apartments for a few months
to a year, but I always ended up back at the house I grew up
in. I can still to this day remember the chills that shot up my
spine when my best friend's mom decided to take me on a
little trip I would like to call the *what you can actually afford*
journey.

She had searched for some rentals in my price range
that she knew I could afford. These were definitely not rentals where I would ever rent, let alone believe that they were
all I could afford. The first few locations were nothing special. But the last one—where I said, "Nope, take me home. I
will live in a box before I live here"—is the one that I'll never
forget. The outside resembled a warehouse, which I thought
was weird, but I went along with it. There was a ramp that
led up to the door and that same ramp I came running down
when I had seen enough. The inside looked like it was an
office with a receptionist's desk. The living room was the
freaking waiting room. Oh, but it gets better. The bedrooms were offices. This building, because I can't even call
it a house, somehow managed to house like ten people. As
we were walking down the hall to check out the bedrooms,
one of the roommates had let out multiple snakes that were
slithering around. Like, were you trying to kill me? I am
scared of snakes! I don't care if that rent was $1 a month. I
wasn't renting there! I never went back to my mom's house
so quick, because if that was what I could technically afford,
then baby, I was going to live at my parents' until I figured
out what to do next!

But finances were only one part of the equation that
I severely lacked knowledge in. My parents did not teach me

about credit or the importance of building it. I was always simply told to *not open up a credit card account*. If you want to live in a world where you don't care about a credit score, than you need to be able to understand how to grow your money and not just spend it the second you receive it. That was a major part of financial literacy that I was not taught. My mom had one credit card, and it was a charge card. She did not mention much about it; I just happened to remember her talking about it once because it was a JC Penney card, a store where she once worked as a very young adult.

When I applied for my first credit card after that car accident I mentioned previously, I did not have good credit. I had made dumb loan purchases through Aarons Furniture Store, took out multiple payday loans, and I had bills in collections. So my first credit card was through First Progress, a credit card that required a down payment. That down payment was my credit limit— $300. I eventually increased it to $500, thinking I was moving in the right direction to build credit. Eventually, I built up my credit enough to have multiple actual credit offers down the line with credit line increases. But I quickly learned that this down payment credit card was not working for me. I ended up paying it off so I could cancel that card and get my $500 back.

Payday loans are something I will never in my life touch again; I consider this predatory lending; they are designed to be conveniently located in low income parts of town because they know broke and uneducated individuals will take the bait. They were conveniently located in the poor small town where I grew up. But they weren't located in the part of town I upgraded to. So that's why I call it predatory because they're purposefully placed in those lower income areas. You end up spending double, if not triple, the amount you paid just a few short weeks later. These are dumber than high interest credit cards, if you ask me, because if you learn to pay your credit card's *full* balance on time, you can avoid paying anything extra. However, some cards have annual fees. Not all cards are the same; some have better rewards and perks than others. But each card is designed to entice you to spend more and more. I started watching finance shows this past year like *Money, Explained* on Netflix and began reading books like *The Black Girl's Guide to Financial Freedom* to help me understand finances better. But what I have learned is that it is completely up to the individual to want to make any necessary changes to their daily habits in order to have an extreme money makeover.

It took me a few years to change my credit and financial situation. But over time and with many different seasons, I was able to do that. It originally involved me working overtime hours to pay off debt, and eventually I used that same tactic to save my extra money. Eventually, I found myself in a place where I could save without working overtime. I highly recommend getting a high-yield savings account where it can just automatically take X amount from every pay check. Eventually, your money makes you extra funds, and you do not have to think twice about remembering to save while doing it. A really good friend and mentor taught me the value of deciding what my baseline budget would become for my monthly bills. That is a major factor of how you go from being broke or living paycheck to paycheck to completely living a different money-saving lifestyle. It's not about the amount of money you make in a year; it's about your bills to income ratio, which is a percentage. So 99 percent spent of any amount leaves you with hardly anything to save. That is what my parents should have showed me. I knew the moment my son thought there was only one bill to pay each month and that the minimum wage was $37 an hour, it was time to educate him. Your future choices will dictate how many bills you have and what kind of hourly rate you will work for. And if you find yourself unhappy with one or the other or even both, every day is a new opportunity to modify your schedule or budget. Budget doesn't necessarily mean less; it simply means *smart*.

Chapter 11: Education and Choosing a Career
Your Education Should Be Your First Investment

In order to save money, you need a job, right? Any job can earn you dollars, but a career can help you excel in life if you know how to use it wisely. Most of us were instructed to go to college and graduate with a degree to get said job. But look at what student loans have done to this country! What if you didn't have someone educating you about this large loan you were about to take on for a degree you would potentially never even use? What if you didn't have someone who told you that those loans will always be expected to be paid back, *even if you declare bankruptcy*!

My high school counselor told me that my "best" option was for me to drop out of high school and get my GED so I could then attend a community college. This was the first of many poor pieces of advice I would be offered. And this right here is exactly why you should question *every* single person who thinks they can tell you what you are worth or capable of. If you went the GED route, no shade there at all. That may have been best for you based on your own personal reasons. But what if I had listened to my high school counselor who thought she knew me better than *me*? Well, I wouldn't be writing this book filled with all of these interesting details, that's for sure.

As you know, I graduated college—three times, to be exact. I knew in my educational journey I did not want to take out student loans unless it became necessary. I had talked to so many nurses in the profession who talked about their student loans of $25,000 or more that they were beginning to repay. In my situation, it just did not make sense for me to take out such a high amount for a degree where I would be making—if I was lucky—$60,000 a year. That's where my research began. I looked into local nursing programs, and I compared the price of the programs to how long it would take me to obtain the degree. There were some accelerated programs, but they were, of course, at private schools, which meant even more money. I decided to do all of my prerequisites at a community college because it was significantly cheaper than a four-year school. Plus, I needed online courses for flexibility in my schedule. This seemed to fit so well for me. I wanted to stay at a community college for an associate's nursing degree because of the price as well. This was such an incredibly great investment because I received a little over $36,000 in Pell Grants, including scholarships, all of which meant *I did not have to pay them back!*

I received scholarships for maintaining good grades and even for being a single mom! The scholarships at this school were endless. I truly do stand behind attending a local community college for your educational needs and goals. Pell Grants are not forever, though; they eventually cap out. Mine luckily lasted through part of getting my bachelor's degree. I then decided to pay out of pocket because I did not want to take out any more loans. I am proud to say I took out less than $7,300 in loans the entire six years I spent in college. My investment in school was well worth it, and it could be for you, too, if you do your own individual research.

Chapter 12: Mental Health and Healing
Don't Be Afraid to Talk About It

Fight or flight—everyone's heard of it. Trauma responses aren't ones that we typically choose to have; they just naturally happen. I learned about my trauma response a long time after I experienced multiple traumas. Mine happens to be freezing up, and I am not a fan. It is a state of mental paralysis. Mine is not so bad that I cannot physically function, but I have come to realize it puts me in a frozen war zone inside my head. I don't have a mirror constantly in front of me, so it's quite possible my friends or family have recognized me in this state, but I wasn't even aware at the time.

I have never liked to openly talk about my true feelings, especially when it comes to the multiple traumas I have endured. If you knew me from thirteen up until twenty-one, all I can really express is how genuinely sorry I am. It's no wonder I was a hot mess during those years. I spent so many days in bed due to a decline in mental health that's why I missed a lot of high school. My mom was unable to get me out of bed. I was angry and sad almost all of the time, despite being able to smile. It is the biggest misconception that a smile means someone is not hurting. Dealing with the loss of my dad with the way it occurred, the following trial that we lost, and the strain it put on the relationship with my mom because of it all, almost broke me. I blamed myself for years that my dad died because I had asked for extra time in the gym that night. I blamed my mom for years for not taking my dad to the hospital, I was *so* upset with her. I was upset with my older siblings for not convincing our mom to call 911. I never truly felt heard even though I knew to my core something was not right and yet no one seemed to believe me. However, I held onto the question of *what if we would have taken him to the hospital the night of the incident?* As a teenager it was hard for me to accept that even if we had taken him to the hospital the night of the accident, the outcome was highly likely to be the same. The reality was that it wasn't any of our faults that he ended up passing away. We didn't cause the accident to begin with.

When I was sixteen, just a few weeks before I found out I was pregnant, my mom took me to a psychiatrist. All I can remember is I cried the entire time as I hated talking to a stranger about my feelings. He diagnosed me with depression and started me on Wellbutrin as a result. I took the pills, but in a few weeks I no longer could take them because I was pregnant. Hormones played a role on my mental health. Not to mention, I tragically lost my biological mom while I was pregnant. I tried really hard to stay positive and be as healthy as I could during that time. I didn't want the physical stress to affect the health of my unborn child during pregnancy. Postpartum played an even larger role on my mental health with the hormones once again. I never felt more imbalanced in my entire life than while I was pregnant and even for a year or two after I had my son. Unfortunately my life was physically up and down just as much as my emotions were. At the time, I didn't have such a strong community behind me as I do now. My friends had graduated high school and had gone their separate ways to attend college. I felt so alone at the time. All I really had was the father of my child, who was also struggling.

Back then my mom had told me that he and I should get married, because then our insurance would be cheaper. Marriage is a beautiful thing if it is shared with the right person. I knew in my heart that was not a reason to get married. I cannot imagine the mental toll that would have been taken on both of us if we had signed up for even more adventures together. But it made me wonder if my mom gave that same poor advice to her other daughters back in the day. Her thought process was that she didn't want me to struggle, especially financially. However, while one may not be struggling to the outside world because they are married under one roof, that doesn't mean they aren't experiencing something else behind closed doors.

I truly don't believe anyone really considered all of the factors I was going through during that time of my life. I knew it was a lot then; it just makes me sad as I look back because I was not given nearly enough grace as I needed. The grief only continued as my journey went on, made worse by working night shift, which played another role in my mental well-being.

Night shift took a toll on me that I really didn't see until I switched to working days. While I was nervous to make such a big change, my mental state was ready. Just a few weeks into working day shift, I was able to really laugh and smile again. I was always told growing up that I was such a joy to be around. Nearly every elementary school teacher would write that for my mom to read at parent-teacher conferences. Now middle school teachers—maybe not so much! But I realized how much of that internal joy I was lacking while working night shift. I will always love the people

I worked with; it takes a special type of person to stay up all night and watch someone else sleep when you are tired. Truly, I don't know which is worse, watching someone sleep when you are tired or watching someone eat when you are hungry. But either way, I am just grateful to be at a point in my life where I no longer feel like I have to be anywhere. Opportunities opened up for me after I moved from night shift to day shift. I only go where I am truly *valued, wanted, and loved*.

Mental health is one thing that has been taken more seriously over the last twenty years in America, but prior to that, you were basically just labeled as being crazy. I truly believe the more we talk about it, the more everyone will realize how *not* alone they truly are. It is so easy to accidentally isolate these days; all it takes is cell phones, tablets, and TV dinner trays. Things humans enjoy in culture are slowly internally killing us. If you put the phone down and pick up a book, you are likely to feel better. And if you put down the tablet and go for a walk outside, you will feel better. Mental health is like going to the gym; results *do not* happen overnight. But if you are *consistent* with whatever routine that *works for you*, over time you will begin to feel and see a huge difference. I found that working out in a more intimate setting instead of a huge gym helped me focus on myself. Its purpose for me was never to lose weight, as many people tend to associate with the gym. For me, it became a space where I could not only focus on my body, but also my mind. I love the concept that HOTWORX created with the small infrared saunas. I sweat more than just the physical toxins out with each HIIT workout. For me, this gym experience became a life-changing routine, more beneficial than any previous memberships I had and never truly used.

But exercise is only part of the equation; the food you choose to consume either elevates or slows you down, especially mentally. Making necessary changes in your diet can sometimes feel impossible. Start with small changes. Limit your unhealthy foods and add healthier ones with each meal. The more you exercise, the healthier you tend to want to eat. I began to feel that change as I took my workout routine more seriously. This routine caused me to reflect and I realized how isolated I had become while living with my ex. He loved to eat dinner on a TV tray and watch *Jersey Shore* religiously, even as an adult in his thirties. And if it wasn't that show, it was something else.

I never wanted to see a TV tray again after my ex, and so when I moved into my own space, I made sure I had a kitchen table. My kitchen table represents community, not isolation. That is where the best open and honest conversations take place with the people I love—with healthier food, might I add.

Chapter 13: Perspectives
Your Mindset Is Your Greatest Asset

I recently watched a TikTok video of a woman of color who shared her experience with a man who tried to have her pay for her own meal at a restaurant. It took me back to my own experience one evening when I was with my ex. He yelled at me in front of my small child because he thought that I did not discipline my son the way he thought I should. He told me that I would have to pay for my own meal. I remember crying, not knowing how to navigate this while strangers were staring at us. I got up from the table with my son after I paid for our meal, and those same strangers asked if I was okay. That's not how a man should *ever* treat a woman in front of her own child. I stand strong and loud on this subject because how men treat women truly does matter, especially when little ones are watching. There is no justification for how that situation was handled that day. If he truly felt that I did not discipline my son the way he thought I should, then that could have just as easily been a conversation with me in private. Then as a result, I would have never had an experience to share years later as I reflect on how that made me feel in that moment as a woman. I could relate to that woman of color in that TikTok. She even shared about how her dad had given her solid advice for dealing with a disrespectful man. I began to wonder how I would have handled that situation differently myself if my own father had not passed when I was thirteen years old and had given me that same solid advice. I didn't have a father who ever yelled at me. He only ever guided me, just as a man should.

When I finally had the courage to share that unfortunate life-changing experience on my social media, I received a message harassing me a day later from a male member of my ex's family. I received that message in my inbox at 1:30 a.m. while I was peacefully sleeping in my new house. As I responded to his message, my ex was a part of a few pages in a few different chapters of my life. But he was not the entire book, as one can now can read. This was *my* story to tell from *my perspective*, based on *my experiences*. The man who sent that message to me ironically *never* witnessed the things I spoke up about and certainly was *not* there during that dinner where I paid for my own meal because I did not discipline my son in the way *my ex saw fit*. This is exactly why so many women do not come forward initially—they are afraid they will not be heard or believed. However, I found my voice, and I stand strong for women who cannot.

I didn't even see what had occurred at the table in order for me to discipline my son right then and there. I needed a moment to process what my ex told me my son had done. He didn't give me the time I needed; he simply began raising his voice at me. Hangry or not, there's still accountability to be had there. Mind you, if you've ever had a four-year-old, you know what they are capable of. No child is perfectly well-behaved when they are hungry, but at the very least, children should be given guidance about why playing with silverware is dangerous. That doesn't have to be yelled for strangers to hear in order for that message to be conveyed to a child.

The male family member who messaged me doesn't have to believe that I am, as he stated, *"mother of the year award there for sure."* He clearly had an opinion. But just know that these words *no longer hurt me or make me feel small.* I was once in a very vulnerable space as a young single mom who needed help. That comment would have normally triggered someone who was not healed which was his goal from the start of that message. However, I now know how to stand up for myself without tearing someone else down in the process. One thing I have come to learn is that a perspective is formed based on *one's actual experiences*; anything else is simply an opinion. If I lived through it I am the *one who experienced it*, which means I have the right to talk about how it affected me. This doesn't mean I am perfect or that I haven't made any mistakes. It actually caused me to look inward because of my experiences. I figured out my own generational curses, and I've made sure I made different choices going forward to correct them. It's only up to you to figure out where your *own* generational curses lie within the male figures in your family. From there, it's up to you to put in the work to change your own behaviors and responses as an adult.

As I've stated in multiple chapters, I'm well aware that I needed help raising my son. I am not afraid to talk about the struggles of being a single mom. My mistake was that I truly once believed I needed a man to do that based on how I was raised, what I saw growing up, and the situation I found myself in. So while one may have the opinion that my ex single-handedly gave me everything I have today, I sure hope after one reads this book that you can see God had other and *bigger plans*, might I add, beyond just a career or a house. Had I stayed in that relationship, I wouldn't have received the blessings I had coming in the format God provided for me.

I became a much better person when I finally lived on my own and began to do the self-work. I didn't just run back to where I was once comfortable, like my ex instructed me to do when I finally had the courage to leave him. That's how I know I broke my own generational curse. It was then that I finally learned that being in a place that was extremely uncomfortable for me only made me gain a new perspective as I faced challenges ahead on my own in my own safe space. That was something that I knew internally that I needed for my personal development as well.

I began doing some modeling in 2023 that led me to do an "into the wild" photoshoot in a creek. It was so hot that day, and my hair was curly for this shoot because I knew I would be getting into the creek. This was the most liberating photoshoot I have ever done. I finally felt so free and comfortable in my own skin for once. But what I didn't know was how much personal strength I was actually showing in that moment. I was getting eaten up by mosquitos because, of course, this photoshoot was in the summertime. While I was posing on the waterfall in the creek, I noticed a black slithering snake around me. A small part of me wanted to scream and run because I am terrified of snakes, but a *larger* part of me wanted to prove to myself that I could do it. I ended up making it through just fine and the photos that were captured by one of my favorite local photographers, Hector's Photography, turned out so well!

My perspective has always been fairly strong. I've had to keep a clear head on these shoulders to persevere through some of the strongest storms. My heart has always loved the beach, and I now have a greater understanding of why. Palm trees were made to bend to survive strong storms; they never break. Strong winds and harsh waves aren't enough to take *my* palm tree down. I have met a ton of people along the way who showed me love and support, and eventually more people who helped nourish my soul. Every now and then I get a patient who leaves a lasting impact on me. I prayed to cross paths with someone who could help guide me in this newer season on my own. And I certainly did; quite a few, actually!

While working as a travel nurse, I got the opportunity to float to other units that I may have never floated to otherwise. One shift, I was floated to an inpatient rehab institute where I crossed paths with a patient who had just been given a terminal diagnosis. This diagnosis was going to affect her ability to walk as it progressed and would eventually lead to her death. She opened up to me about how she truly felt about it as this had left her devastated. I ended up crying at the bedside with her as she told me how she had all of these plans to take trips and wear these cute shoes she had already bought. Now she was facing a devastating challenge to even walk, so the shoes would become pointless as she replaced them with mobility boots and a wheelchair. I told her to just wear the shoes anyway for the pictures. She could still have that memory that she dreamed of while taking those pictures as she was quite literally living like the song, "Live Like You Were Dying," by Tim McGraw.

A mutual friend kept me updated about her prognosis and travels across the country as her illness progressed. My heart is so full just knowing that she got the opportunity to travel and mark off a few things on her bucket list that she told me about—I hope she still wore those shoes. Because she opened up to me about her diagnosis, I opened up to her about my life. Funny enough, I'll never forget her initial first question after I was done talking. She was shocked at how far I had come and even more shocked at my answer that followed. She asked, "Did you get therapy?" My answer was no, I did not. However, I was still able to tell her many months after this encounter that she helped inspire me to write this book!

Another good friend who became a mentor to me taught me how valuable a shift of perspective can be. The truth is, how you view your entire life can be the reason why you stay down or get back up. Everyone gets dealt different cards, but everyone gets a *choice* at some point as well. Some of the cards I was dealt are relatable in one way or another, and maybe not all of them are applicable to you. But I do truly believe there is power in choosing to use your pain for something better. Every day is a new opportunity for a new perspective; you are never complacent unless you want to be. You are never too old to learn. And you certainly are never too old to grow. There is not one single person who could take complete credit for me surviving every storm and season God had intended for me to go through. But I appreciate the community he gave me to help me along the way. I finally found my purpose even through all of that pain, so I know firsthand that you absolutely can too. That is *my* legacy I am passing on. May God bless the reader's hands who picked up this book and extend that blessing to someone else who needs it.

Acknowledgments

I want to first thank God for the opportunity to still be here to write this book filled with all of the unique details that made me who I am today. Thank you to my biological parents for bringing me into this world, and thank you to my parents, who adopted and raised me to the best of their abilities. Thank you to my best friend, who is like a sister to me, for always encouraging me to keep going despite the many traumas I faced, never leaving my side even when life took us opposite directions, and subsequently moving over a thousand miles away. Thank you to my best friend's mom, who is like another mother to me—I don't think I'll ever be able to tell you thank you enough for all that you did for me over the years. Thank you to my son for teaching me the importance of patience and understanding. A big thank-you to my good friend and mentor for really challenging me to understand myself when my life finally calmed down enough for me to examine my life through another lens. Thank you to my half sisters on both sides of my family—I value our sisterhood for all of the similarities and differences I have learned to embrace and celebrate with you. Thank you to my older adopted siblings for showing me love throughout all of the years. Thank you to my friends in so many different eras of my life who helped me overcome some really dark times, and if you stuck around, an even bigger round of applause. Thank you to the many educators, coworkers, and even patients who provided guidance or advice, challenged me, and encouraged me to keep going.

Last but not least, I'd like to say thank you to the select few who gave me unsettling advice or told me I couldn't do it. I've always loved a good challenge; I might bend, but I'll *never* break.

About the Author

Kristina Davidson, author of *The Power Of Using Pain For Purpose,* is a beacon of resilience and empowerment. Overcoming early traumas, including the loss of her parents, Kristina defied the odds—graduating college and buying her first home as a single mom. Navigating the challenges of a tough housing market and a global pandemic during her nursing career, she found strength and renewed faith. Kristina's journey explores trauma, adoption, culture, generational curses, and wavering faith. Through her book, she becomes a bold advocate for unheard women's voices, offering an inspiring tale of triumph against all odds through faith, family, and friends.